T0331096

Security Awareness Design in the New Normal Age

People working in our cyber world have access to a wide range of information including sensitive personal or corporate information which increases the risk to it. One of the aspects of protection of this data is to train the user to behave more securely. This means that every person who handles sensitive information, their own or that of other people, be aware of the risks that their use can pose as well as how to do their job in such a way as to reduce that risk. The approach we use for that is called 'security awareness' but would be more accurately described as security 'unawareness' because most of the problems come where the user doesn't know about risk from their behaviour or its potential impact. In these post-COVID days of 'New Normal' working, in which staff spend more of their time working at home, organisations are still responsible for the protection of sensitive personal and corporate data. This means that it is more important than ever to create an effective security awareness communication process. This book will primarily consider the problem of hitting that 'Sweet Spot' in the age of 'New Normal' working, which means that the knowledge about secure practice is not only understood and remembered but also reliably put into practice – even when a person is working alone. This will be informed by academic research as well as experience, both my own and learnt from my fellow professionals, and then will be used to demonstrate how 'New Normal' working can improve security awareness as well as challenge it.

Security Awareness Design in the New Normal Age

Wendy F. Goucher

CRC Press
Taylor & Francis Group
Boca Raton   London

CRC Press is an imprint of the
Taylor & Francis Group, an **informa** business

First edition published 2023
by CRC Press
6000 Broken Sound Parkway NW, Suite 300, Boca Raton, FL 33487–2742

and by CRC Press
4 Park Square, Milton Park, Abingdon, Oxon, OX14 4RN

CRC Press is an imprint of Taylor & Francis Group, LLC

Library of Congress Cataloging-in-Publication Data
Names: Goucher, Wendy, author.
Title: Security awareness design in the new normal age / Wendy F. Goucher.
Description: First edition. | Boca Raton : CRC Press, 2022. | Includes
    bibliographical references and index.
Identifiers: LCCN 2022001842 (print) | LCCN 2022001843 (ebook) |
    ISBN 9781032047645 (hardback) | ISBN 9781032047652 (paperback) |
    ISBN 9781003194583 (ebook)
Subjects: LCSH: Computer security. | Computer networks—Security measures. |
    Risk Communication. | Risk perception. | Organizational behavior.
Classification: LCC QA76.9.A25 G675 2022 (print) | LCC QA76.9.A25 (ebook) |
    DDC 005.8—dc23/eng/20220422
LC record available at https://lccn.loc.gov/2022001842
LC ebook record available at https://lccn.loc.gov/2022001843

ISBN: 978-1-032-04764-5 (hbk)
ISBN: 978-1-032-04765-2 (pbk)
ISBN: 978-1-003-19458-3 (ebk)

DOI: 10.1201/9781003194583

Typeset in Caslon
by Apex CoVantage, LLC

Contents

Acknowledgement

I would like to thank Alasdair Pemble and Cate Pemble for their work in editing this book.

Introduction

Common Sense . . . Isn't

Modern businesses run on information. Every service, every product, every interaction or transaction, and every employee are recorded somewhere.

It makes sense, then, for modern businesses to consider not only the physical security of their assets but the digital security of their information. Some may even argue that taking steps to ensure information security, and security awareness, is common sense. But is it? And is common sense really that simple — or that common?

It will come as no surprise to anyone reading this book when I say that the way we work, have worked and will work has changed drastically over recent years. Whether we are talking about increasingly powerful personal devices, access to WiFi in public spaces, or the ability to continue working and connecting with colleagues even when we're sitting on a plane travelling 550 miles an hour, 40,000 feet in the air, our working practices are evolving. Indeed, this process of moving away from the traditional on-site desk-tethered mode of working may be the greatest change in generalised working styles since the development of the production line!

But have our security practices kept up with these changes? Do people understand the steps they need to take to make sure they can work securely while travelling, or sitting in a café, or even working from home? The honest answer is 'probably not', and that's a problem – after all, advanced password protection software means nothing if people are still writing their passwords on Post-it® notes and taping them to their screen or keeping them in a word document on their desktop.

This is why one of the most important steps in improving information security practices is training the user so that they use and understand secure working practices. But this is no small task, it means training every person who handles sensitive information of any kind, to make sure they have the information and the skills necessary to use

DOI: 10.1201/9781003194583-1

a variety of tools and techniques to reduce the risk of data breach, or data loss. The official name for this approach is security awareness, and it is the direct opposite of the thoughtless, foolish or dangerous practices that 'security ignorance' can bring.

But why read this book now? If the world of work has been changing for years, with the availability of more advanced computers and more mobile working, why read *this* book *now?*

The answer is simple. This book has been written during and for the COVID-19 pandemic and beyond. As I write this foreword in the Autumn of 2021, industries and companies from across the globe are struggling to adapt to a 'New Normal' working pattern that involves more working from home, more flexibility and less reliance on a shared physical office space within which everyone works, securely or insecurely, together.

This has brought with it several challenges, especially in regard to ensuring security and data privacy. For example, many of the more traditional methods for reminding people about good security practices, such as hanging posters, leaving messages on notepads and (if all else fails) the time-honoured shoulder tap whereby a colleague reminds you to lock your screen as you leave your desk, have been lost in the shift from corporate to the domestic working environments. So, the question becomes, how can we help people to understand and follow secure working practices when we are not always physically present together? How can processes and procedures be reviewed and revised to remain fit for purpose in the 'New Normal' era? How do we find that 'sweet spot' where people are about to take on board new messages and techniques to become more security-aware, without overloading or overwhelming them? How do we get the message into the heads of busy people so that they not only remember it when they need to but also when working securely becomes a habit that they don't need to think about?

The question, then, is not only "how can we fix the unsafe working habits that people have developed during COVID-19" but "how can we recognise and build on the things that we've learned during this time".

The first step is communication. I've been 'banging the drum' for years about the importance of communicating with staff around information and cybersecurity, arguing that it was important to not only teach people 'what' to do, but why they should, and what the impact might be if they didn't, both for them as an individual and for the wider team or business. I argue that people will be more inclined to change their behaviour if they can personally see, or experience, a benefit from that behaviour. I called this teaching *'Selfish Security'* and it has been something that has been well received by academic and industrial communities alike. The difficulty comes, however, when we try and move from this approach being a "good idea" to actually update training and working practices. After all, good security awareness, and solid security practices, only show up on the balance sheet as a cost, an investment or a *lack* of a catastrophic problem, and that can be difficult to justify to budget holders at the best of times.

I have worked with several organisations over the last two years. I have watched as we moved from early COVID working practices, balancing laptops on ironing boards and sofa cushions, to the more refined processes of the 'New Normal' era. I have seen and heard the different ways in which people in a variety of industries were challenged by the COVID pandemic, witnessing the range of skills they have developed in response. They often had to develop skills alone or under-supported, as every person around them tried desperately to do the same. This book is a combination of their stories and expertise, as well as my own professional knowledge and a hefty dose of academic and business research, drawn together so that we can learn from all areas of research and practice to grow together.

I firmly believe that there are good lessons that we can salvage from this time. In fact, I think it's important that we do so, because while many of us have tried to recognise and thank those frontline workers, healthcare providers and social services staff who played a vital role in helping us all through this crisis, they are not the only people who were instrumental to our success. Indeed, it's important to remember that while this book functions by shining a light on common issues and gaps in security awareness and suggesting practical, sustainable and scalable solutions, this is only possible *because* we know that good practices exist and we know what they look like. Many organisations and their staff have achieved amazing things during these last 18 months, with little recognition or applause. I'm not talking about people who were regularly (and rightly!) celebrated during this pandemic, but those who worked, often invisibly and tirelessly, behind the scenes to make remote working possible. People who took care of huge computer systems and data clouds and those who worked to meet the increasing digital threats posed by ransomware packages, for example, without whom our New Normal would not have been possible. Some of those people have worked to breaking point just so we had the infrastructure to continue to work safely as the pandemic progressed, and it's important to recognise their contribution to us all.

With that in mind, I would like to take this opportunity to thank several people for their help in writing this book. After all, if the last two years have taught us anything, it is surely to value one another and never leave a positive word or compliment unsaid. Therefore, I would like to thank all of those invisible people for their work over this chaotic period. Much of what we have achieved together over these last years would not have been possible without you. I would also like to thank my family for their support while writing this book, especially Alasdair and Cate, who provided a second pair of eyes when I needed them, and Matthew, who provided nearly endless cups of tea and much-needed support on a daily basis.

Wendy F. Goucher

1
WHAT IS SECURITY AWARENESS AND WHY SHOULD YOU CARE?

Introduction

The word 'holistic' is one that is commonly used these days, especially in relation to approaches to healthcare. However, we can also use it to understand a wide range of awareness and behaviour, both on a computer and off that impacts the protection of data. In short, security awareness should be part of a holistic understanding of Information and Cyber Security, not a poor cousin that is relegated as less important, until a situation occurs where greater awareness could have protected or mitigated the impact. As someone who came into the profession via interest in security awareness, I have been cheered to see a growth in its incorporation into more mainstream information security.

That said, I think it is important to use this first chapter to both explain security awareness and consider where it fits with operational practices in organisations before we move on to look at the impact of working through COVID times has made. In doing so, I will also share some examples of where incidents, some well-known in the public domain, have demonstrated where relatively straightforward raising of security awareness would clearly reduce some significant, and in one case, very embarrassing impacts.

While much of this book is going to focus on the future, and how individuals and organisations can act now to become increasingly secure as time goes on, we need to understand where we came from if we are going to map out our route to security awareness moving forward.

Let's start by talking about what we mean when we talk about security awareness.

DOI: 10.1201/9781003194583-2

First and foremost, we should acknowledge that 'security aware-ness' is a bit of a misnomer. It doesn't accurately describe what we're talking about, or even what we're trying to do.

Start with the word 'security,' for example. This is a strong, concrete word that sends a clear message: after all to be secure is to be in a place of protection, often behind defences designed to keep threats at bay. It conjures images of strong walls and deep hidden vaults, dedicated to protecting valuable things. This makes sense to us as we think about the information we store. If data is precious, we think, then of course we should, to borrow a phrase, "keep it secret, keep it safe".

So, what about 'awareness'? Why do we need to be aware of secu-rity? After all, strong walls and deep vaults don't need our constant attention to be secure! I think about this often and wonder what peo-ple think security professionals mean when we say they need to be *aware* of information security. Do they think we're asking them to know who manages information security in their business, or know that information needs to be secure? Or do they think about their role in security as a process? After all, neither walls nor vaults can protect against threats if they are left open. Precious things might stop being safe, if they are not kept secret – and who knows what long road may lie ahead to fix a problem brought about by indiscretion. It reminds me of the Second World War adage; 'loose lips sink ships', because while the scale is different, the principle remains the same.

This is why security awareness needs to include an awareness of why a secure process is required in the first place. The "why" is impor-tant. I often find myself thinking about my children when I present this concept, drawn back into my memories of the toddler years where every other word out of their mouth seemed to be "why". Why was the response to every instruction, every statement and every event large or small – whether I was prepared to answer it or not? Understanding the reasoning behind a rule can help children understand why it exists and help them to remember to do (or not do!) something whether their parent is in the room or not. Without the 'why', children can't learn that they just shouldn't do *this thing* or say *that thing* in front of a particular person, rather than that they shouldn't do or say something in general. The same logic applies with security awareness – without understanding the 'why' of a particular policy or practice, staff may choose to ignore it as long as they're out of sight, presenting a security risk in the process. This is even more important to think about now so many of us are working remotely, or in blended pattern, where we are often 'out of sight'.

This doesn't mean that the "why" questions around our security practices will always be comfortable or easy to answer. In fact, "why?" is one of the most difficult questions to prepare for, especially when we are trying to get people to change their behaviour, but we shut down that conversation at our peril. It is the why that helps staff understand the importance of their behaviour, and sometimes, the why that makes us think again about our own security practices by prompting us to think about something from a new, and unanticipated, angle.

So, making staff aware of security means not only educating them about the kinds of security in place but their role in it. There is no use in providing half of the information when people need to understand the *why* as well as the *what*. They need to understand the risk or threat and what they must do to recognise how important their own actions are in maintaining that security. This is traditionally achieved through formal, scheduled training: where a designated person takes on the role of communicating important rules and guidelines to staff in order to inform and empower them to work in a way that protects sensitive information. But this overt training isn't the only option available, and there are several techniques that organisations can use to nudge, prompt or remind people to behave in the right way without interrupting their daily workflow. We'll talk about some of these techniques in later chapters.

So, security awareness is about understanding that a threat or risk exists, knowing that there are steps that a person can take to help protect sensitive information and systems, and putting that knowledge into practice. Laying it out this way makes security awareness sound simple, or at least straightforward; identify a threat and build a defence to counter it, but things are rarely so clean in the real world. The fact you are reading in this book means you probably already know that. So what's the problem? Why isn't security awareness as straightforward in practice as it is in theory? One reason is the hidden complexity that hides between the steps of "identify the threat" and "the person takes preventive action". Because, in fact, the sequence of events includes the identification of the threat, *designing the defence, motivating the defender,* and that defender acting to mitigate potential security risks.

Practicality

An effective security campaign or procedure is one that accounts for the day-to-day working practices and behaviours of the people it is trying to influence. Indeed, we often see this as a key failing when looking at unsuccessful initiatives after the fact, as we realise that the proposed solution unintentionally added stress or burden onto the people who were required to implement it. This additional level of burden can then lead to people ignoring or avoiding the new, more secure practices, as they actively get in the way of their ability to complete their work and meet their targets.

Example

In the early 2010s, an NHS Health Board raised concerns regarding the security of paper-based patient records when nurses were visiting patients in the community. There was a concern that taking patient records into the community might lead to a healthcare practitioner leaving sensitive documents behind after a visit, resulting in unauthorised people having access to sensitive information.

Several potential solutions were considered. One proposal suggested that staff should simply leave all documentation that was not relevant to a particular visit locked in their car. This then led to the concern of the data being lost or leaked if the car should be stolen while the healthcare practitioner was visiting a patient. This is a valid concern, as it doesn't matter whether getting access to the documents was on the mind of the thief when they stole the car, it only matters that stealing the car would result in the loss of that information.

With this in mind, the Health Board took the suggestion a step further, and redesigned the process to ensure that practitioners only ever carried the files of the patient they were visiting at any time. All other files would remain in that practitioner's central hub. This appeared to solve the problem entirely, as no papers would be left unattended in a car (and thus potentially stolen), and the patient would only have access to their own records should any paperwork be forgotten or left behind by the healthcare practitioner after the visit.

What this proposal didn't consider was the practical implications of this solution. To work 'securely' under these new procedures, healthcare practitioners would have to return to their central hub between every patient visit, to return the files of the patient they had just seen and collect the paperwork for their next visit. In practice, this could have a significant effect on workflow, especially if the community being served was rural or widespread, with patients living further away from the central hub. This could be particularly frustrating when healthcare practitioners were visiting several patients in the same location, such as in a nursing home, as they would have to leave and return to the same location multiple times to comply with the new procedure. More time being spent in transit meant that healthcare practitioners would have to spend less time with each patient or visit less frequently to make up for the lost time.

Ultimately, these solutions were considered unworkable, and the risk was flagged as an ongoing issue, with the task of risk mitigation being delegated to the different surgeries, hubs, and practitioners to allow a tailored solution that worked for their situation.

This example allows us to see the importance of creating security practices and solutions that recognise the practical day-to-day aspects of an organisation that are sensitive to the resources available at the time. For instance, the earlier example has long since been improved, as paper records were replaced by digital records, which allows healthcare practitioners to have access to a range of patient files using their mobile device – so the risk of files being left anywhere is no more. Yet, with this advancement comes new concerns about device security, encryption and shoulder surfing, and so the process of threat recognition, defence design, motivation and secure practices continues.

Insecurity Awareness

So why did I say that security awareness was a misnomer and doesn't reflect the issues at hand? After all, don't we want staff to be aware of security processes, follow them and thereby protect data? Well, of course we do, but I would argue that many issues around information security occur not when individuals fail to be aware of the security procedures in place but when they fail to recognise moments of *insecurity*. Becoming aware of areas of insecurity is a vital step in making information more secure. Staff need to recognise not only the procedures in place but the world of potential risks to data and, importantly, an absence of security measures to counter them. In short, we need 'insecurity awareness'.

Human Insecurity Awareness and the Media

The thing is that insecurity awareness isn't as difficult to spread as you might think. Long ago, in the misty days of 2008, a series of news stories in the UK elevated information security to the general public consciousness. No longer was the only risk to information some strange techno-magic devised in dark corners by illusive hackers wearing black hoodies and typing inexplicably quickly. Instead, the public became aware of the risk associated with human action or inaction.

Example

On 18 October 2007, Her Majesty's Revenue and Customs Office (HMRC) received a legitimate request for information about the recipients of child benefits. This request included, but was not limited to, the names and addresses of everyone in receipt of that benefit. This information was collected was burned onto two CDs, which were then sealed in an envelope and sent by unrecorded internal mail to the National Audit Office.

On 24 October the National Audit Office complained that the HMRC had not responded to their request as no data had arrived. It seems likely that what followed was a period of some panic. An enquiry was formed, reviewing everything from whether the discs had indeed been burned as stated, to a physical check of every building that the discs would have passed through. Cupboards and filing cabinets were searched, as the efforts to locate the discs moved beyond the HMRC offices, to the post office centres that might have handled the envelope, and beyond.

The search was unsuccessful, for while the enquiry could show that the discs had indeed been created, and that they had been prepared for posting, their whereabouts after this point were unknown. The error was not with the HMRC, but somewhere on the journey between the HMRC and the National Audit Office. The Chancellor of the Exchequer was briefed of the data loss on November 10th, and what followed was a wealth of news coverage about the most famous and widespread data security leak in the UK up to that point. After all, child benefit was not means tested in 2011, and the discs therefore contained the names and addresses of almost every child under the age of 18 in the UK. There were additional fears, too, as the bank details of many families had been recorded on those discs, where those families had chosen to receive child benefit straight into an account rather than through other means.

The media coverage that followed leak was widespread, and every affected home in the country received a letter from the government explaining the events. And thus, almost overnight, approximately 25 million people in the UK learned how easy it was for their data to become compromised through the actions of people they didn't know and would never meet.

With data loss the focus of the moment, journalists began to search for more examples of data leaks caused by human error. After all, there was little hay to be made of an anonymous hacker, working in complex and mysterious ways half a world away – but a human assisted data leak, that had potential. Human assisted data loss could have a name, and an opportunity to assign blame and seek justice. Suddenly, the abstract concept of 'data loss' could have a face.

Examples like these may seem obvious in hindsight, but it is important that human-assisted data loss is not just about making careless mistakes, like leaving a laptop on a train or sending sensitive information to the wrong person. In fact, many instances of this type of data loss occur simply because no one has ever considered the potential threat before. Consider, for example, the case of a UK bank upgrading their computers in 2008 and passing their old machines to a third party for secure disposal, only for those same machines to appear on eBay sometime later, hard drives intact. Data, potentially sensitive, was recoverable by anyone with access to the machines and the tools to do so. Such incidents spawned changes in practice around how old machines are disposed of, but I do wonder how far this awareness goes. Do photocopiers, with their own dedicated hard drives, get the same treatment, for example? Or do they get disposed of or sold along without a thought?

Taking precautions to protect against some of these avenues of data loss is one of the easiest ways in which an organisation can become more security, or insecurity, aware. After all, it's easy enough to upgrade a piece of office technology without thinking too deeply about the exact details of how it works, but this convenience comes at a cost. Sometimes the cost is people's sensitive data and the media flurry that follows – after all, it was a recognisable bank with the established brand that found itself at the centre of the media storm, not the negligent third party.

In Plain Sight

Insecurity awareness is a funny thing. It is easy for routine and habit to cloud our awareness of the risks of data loss as we go about our daily lives, only to suddenly recognise the threat when it is pointed out to us. This is a concept I explored while conducting my master's research while exploring the phenomenon of shoulder surfing. Shoulder surfing is, in short, the ability of people to access other people's data by glancing at, or taking pictures of, someone else's screen in a public place. This is another example of the ongoing process of security awareness, after all, shoulder surfing would have been far more difficult in the 80s or 90s, whereas it's now possible for people to work from their handheld devices or laptops almost anywhere, in real time, as increasing memory capacity and the ability to access cloud storage or VPN protected networks makes it as easy to work from home, or local café, as in the office. With such opportunities come new threats, and the chance the secure information will become accessible to the person one table over, if they only glance at the laptop someone is working on.

The following incident was described to me in 2011, just as I was beginning my academic research:

> *A lady sat next to me [on the train] with a pile of papers. These were all written in a large font – maybe 18. When the conductor came, she had some problems finding her ticket, so she passed a pile of papers to me, well put them on my keyboard, while she looked. The top was the transcript of and e-mail between (Company A) and another organisation about how an enforcement notice was going to be enacted. She was clearly the (Company A) person. The page had her name and her contact details on it- as well as all the business details.*

And that's how easy it is for a lack of insecurity awareness to become a loss of sensitive data, because I have disguised the name of Company A in the account quoted earlier, but in actuality, the observer knew the identity of both parties, as well as some information about the contents of the document. All at a glance, and all, likely, without the woman at her side even realising the data had been compromised. Now imagine this occurred not in 2011, but in 2021, with the widespread availability of high-zoom, high-resolution cameras in most smartphones, and the potential for data loss becomes even more apparent.

The crucial point here is that, despite information security's association with IT, no piece of security software could have prevented this simple act of human error. Many instances of data leakage aren't even detected until an eagle-eyed person spots an open document or unlocked screen in a photograph once it's uploaded.

That potential isn't hypothetical, either. Indeed, one of the most famous examples of this happened earlier, in 2009, when the Assistant Commissioner of the Metropolitan Police Service, Robert Quick was photographed by reporters leaving Downing Street with a sheath of documents in his hand. These contained sensitive information regarding planned antiterror operations and were quickly broadcast across international news platforms outlets (albeit after some careful censoring).

The impact for Robert Quick was significant; antiterror operations had to be drastically altered and Quick considered tending his own resignation.

In another case, this time in 2012, while HRH Prince William was serving in the Royal Air Force, selected members of the press were allowed into the office where he and his colleagues worked. It was a relaxed photo which seemed to show the prince and his colleagues relaxed and happy while at work. It was not until the pictures were examined later that someone noticed that was a note pinned to the wall with a username and password. While most of the media edited the words out, a quick search on the internet found the original pictures. It was later reported that the password was for an online game, not any form of military files or software, but the potential damage from such leaks remains significant.

This is why it is important to talk about insecurity awareness and promote insecurity awareness, because errors like these are often entirely avoidable. For example, participants who had contributed to my research by recording instances of people working insecurely in public places often reported being more aware of their own working behaviour, changing their habits as a result. Such is the power of turning an abstract concept like security awareness into an applied exercise that people can do for themselves whenever and wherever they go. We'll talk more about how you can leverage this in your own organisations in Chapter 5, but for now, it is enough to recognise that people need to be aware of risk before they will be motivated to act to mitigate it. This means that the people designing and delivering training need to be aware too.

Governance and Compliance

The ISO standard 270001, which was first launched in 2005, guided organisations to take a more holistic view of security and consider aspects relating to the non-technical processing of information. Its publication was influential then not just in laying out new standards of security but in signalling an end to the days when 'information security' was solely the problem of the IT department. Following its publication, in order to comply with the standard organisations had to recognise that responsibility and accountability rested primarily at board level. Indeed organisations needed to consider all situations where potentially sensitive material was processed and ensure that their policies, procedures and controls were sufficiently robust to provide protection to data from risk of loss or corruption. This was later followed by other legislation, like the General Data Protection Regulation (GDPR) (ICO 2017), which placed significant emphasis on the way data is used, stored and disposed of.

There is, therefore, significant legal and regulatory pressure on organisations and individuals to improve the protection of sensitive data, and we've already established that secure procedures must be accompanied by increased security, or insecurity, awareness across all staffing levels. This awareness helps to ensure that people continue to follow secure practices when working away from the office and outside the scope of direct monitoring by colleagues and seniors. This might mean working at home, or in a local library, or something more extreme, such as working while abroad, particularly while visiting family or staying in a communal space. Here the issues around data security are not only the mundane, familiar issues around people physically seeing your data or your password but complex issues of governance and security that can prohibit people from accessing or working on certain data while overseas. This is especially common if they are visiting a country with a high rate of cybercrime, where there are known activities ongoing to collect data or launch malware or ransomware attacks. Staff often do not consider this when preparing for a visit abroad and might be surprised to learn that taking their work with them is counter to good security practice. I have to hope that most learn of this via a stern conversation with a professional within their organisation and not, as in the cases of some of the organisations I work with, by attempting to log into a work system from a remote location only to have their machine wiped as part of the organisations' security protocol.

Importantly, I'd argue that the blame for incidents like these does not lie with the individual alone, but the individual worker, their manager, and their security team, all of whom should have played a role in ensuring that the worker was sufficiently educated to become security, or insecurity, aware.

You and Your Staff Are the 'Weakest Links'

It seems like no conversation about information or cybersecurity, and the role of humans within it, is complete without dipping into the works of Bruce Schneier. I always recommend that those interested in the world of information security read his work, beginning with his first book, 'Secrets & Lies: Digital Security in a Networked World' (2000) and 'Beyond Fear: Thinking Sensibly About Security in an Uncertain World' (2003), the latter of which was originally recommended to me as "a book that should be put into the hand of every CEO before they made a long-haul flight".

The most famous of Schneier's quotes, which is so popular it has almost become an adage at this point, is that *people often represent the weakest link in the security chain*" (Schneier, 2000). I can see why the sentiment might be popular, too, as in just ten words it can shift the onus for information security away from computers and IT systems, and back to the individual user. It becomes, in essence, a get out of jail free card for everyone *but* the user. This allows money to be spent on expensive and intricate systems without too much concern, as any incidents that might occur because of the way that people use that system are viewed exclusively as the fault of that individual. The end user therefore becomes the scapegoat carrying any technical mistakes or issues with practicality away, leaving the technical professionals who commissioned, designed or maintained the system without any need to adapt the existing framework. It was, after all, user error.

I have seen Bruce Schneier speak on a number of occasions, however, and I have never been left with the impression of a man wedded to some pessimistic 'we are all doomed so there's no point in trying to fix the humans' attitude. As a result, I, like others, don't agree with any interpretation of the quote that places the burden of responsibility exclusively on the shoulders of end users. I believe that phrase was intended to be a call to action to address any area of weakness that is discovered whether that is through effort or investment at an individual or organisational level. It's not enough to say that the individual did not use a tool in the way it was intended, we have to look at why, what issues or challenges prompted them to use this tool that way, and address those, too.

We must, then, always consider the 'human factor' in our security protocols. A tool that does not serve its end user well will, after all, often be adapted or used in ways that were not intended. It will take time and effort but, with the right training, the human can transform, shifting from being the 'weakest link' to a flexible and adaptive defender of precious information.

2

SECURITY AWARENESS AND PROTECTING INFORMATION THROUGH HISTORY

Introduction

Especially as we now work in a world where even industries such as forestry, a subject that is largely focused on the outdoor situation, use the digital input and processing of information, it is tempting to regard information security as being something that is part of our modern age – maybe with its genesis with the 'codebreakers' in the Second World War at Bletchley Park. However, this would be to miss out on the contribution both to the obfuscation and to the revealing of secrets that stretches back to the earliest days of written communication. So, to follow the observation by Sir Winston Churchill, Britain's wartime prime minister and historian, "Those who ignore history are doomed to repeat it", this chapter will give a tour of some highlights of information security and awareness through history. I will then identify a number of situations that can be defended by awareness and 'common sense' that our ancestors used to defend themselves.

One of the key tenants of effective security awareness is that both the message as it is received and the behaviour as it is practiced must be meaningful to the end user. Considering a modern, pre-COVID office, for example, chances are that many of the controls that were in place to protect both information and staff were based on a technology. For several of the organisations I've worked for, this has looked something like installing 'bump and pin' doors between different zones, which require staff needing to present their card and enter their PIN number to gain access to the area beyond. Installing this sort of security can result in a variety of changes, for example, making the outer doors bump and pin removed the need for a receptionist at the main door.

DOI: 10.1201/9781003194583-3

The question that should be considered when such opportunities appear, however, is not just *can* a change be made but *should* a change be made. In this case, was handing out visitor badges really the only role the receptionist played? I would argue that the role was more important than that. Yes, a receptionist provided a friendly face to greet visitors and provide directions, but they also offered an additional layer of security, as a physical set of eyes that would see anyone unexpectedly entering or moving around the building. Shifting away from this human element and relying on technological security alone introduces a range of potential issues, including questions about what happens if the security system fails, is bypassed or simply loses power. It raises other issues too, as staff may assume that anyone within the bump and pin zone has permission to be there and stop challenging strangers when they appear unexpectedly in these spaces.

They can, in effect, 'turn off' their awareness of a potential stranger and let the technology take the strain. After all, if people have been able to get through the door unescorted then they must have an authenticating card – what need is there to challenge them?

But we know that there are simple ways to bypass card entry systems such as by 'tailgating' someone entering ahead of you, or pretending you've left your card at your desk and asking a helpful soul to let you in 'just this once'. These 'social engineering' approaches work because people have been trained to trust technology before their own judgement, and while this might be convenient for us as individuals, it represents a major threat to information security.

It is important then that we acknowledge that information security, and security awareness, existed long before modern information technology. Indeed, human-led security is the ancestor of today's information security profession, so let's consider the lessons we can learn from our history before we forge ahead and risk reinventing a (albeit digital) wheel.

Obfuscation

Obfuscation, or the practice whereby we hide or encrypt information, is not a new practice. At its peak, the Roman Empire covered a great deal of Europe, North Africa and even parts of what are now the Middle East. Yet an empire this vast meant a variety of issues,

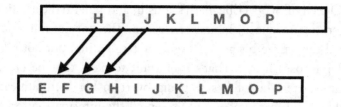

including how to communicate clearly across long distances. There are a number of issues to consider when talking about communication, one of the most obvious is speed, but there is also the not-so-small matter of making sure a message can reach the right person without the information being captured or changed by hostile entities.

So it goes that the 'Caesar Cypher' (and other, less catchily named methods) was born. The cypher worked like this, with each letter of the message being substituted for another at a specific interval elsewhere in the alphabet. Caesar's specific cypher reportedly used letters three steps behind the correct one, as in the following image.

While simplistic and easily broken by others within Caesar's court, it served to protect messages from random encounters with enemy forces.

Some historians have theorised that hostile forces might simply view a message written in cypher as one that was written in a language they were not familiar with and as such make no attempt to break the code. Some might mischievously suggest that the notoriously unreadable handwriting of family doctors was possibly unintentionally a cypher of its own. The Caesar Cypher continued down the years, with Caesar's nephew, Augustus, adding his own variation where each letter was shifted one step to the right, alongside thousands of other variations using a similar mechanism.

Nor were such early methods of data encryption limited to the Roman Empire. A notable example is the appearance of England's first official 'Spymaster' Sir Francis Walsingham (1532–1590), who served under Queen Elizabeth I. Of course, Walsingham differs from Caesar in several ways, but one of the most important for our purposes is that he not only devised cyphers to communicate with agents across Europe but actively sought to break the cyphers of others and employed a team of scholars specifically for this task. This was, of course, key to his success, as Walsingham worked to catch

Mary Queen of Scots (Elizabeth's cousin, and potential catholic rival to the protestant queen) in acts of treason. The story of quite how he managed to achieve his goal is arguably fascinating, but not relevant for our purposes here. What's important to us is that he created a situation where Mary felt safe being overt in her communications, worked to break her cypher and presented the information to Queen Elizabeth I. His work led to the execution of both Mary and Anthony Babington, to whom she was writing.

For a more recent example, we can look at the Second World War communication with people behind enemy lines. Many of these approaches were extremely creative such as a set of clothing designed to function as a secret, wearable codebook or the 'one-time pad' where each message used passed a different encryption code. The latter was obviously safer as it is arguably harder to intercept a message you don't have the cypher to decode, than it is to steal someone's jacket. You do have to respect the sheer drama and style of the wearable option, however.

Perhaps the most famous examples of early 'information security' comes from the tales around the code machines used by the German military, the Lorenz machine, and its famous counterpart, Enigma. Enigma utilised moving parts in its transmitting machine, adjusting the cypher with every use and effectively hampering allied attempts to decipher intercepted messages. Eventually, some of these machines were captured and their mechanisms studied, yet decryption of these messages remained a major obstacle.

Earlier versions of Enigma had been combatted by Polish cryptologist Marian Rejewski and his 'Bomba' device before the Second World War had even begun, and it was this design that Alan Turing would later build upon, producing the British 'Bombe' in 1939. Turing's machine was ultimately used to counter the Enigma. Yet here, too, we can see the hand of human habit and the role of humans in data loss. Turing and his team noticed that messages often opened with news about the weather, and so 'wetter' became a useful keyword with which allied cryptologists could deduce the positions of the cogs on the German transmission machine at the time of broadcast. The victory, then, was built brick by brick on top of these small, almost benign human habits, which ultimately lead to triumph over the Enigma's mechanisms.

Separation and Access Control

So why consider our history when we talk about information security? Well, it is first and foremost to combat this idea that information security is a new or unique aspect of the 21st century. Instead, we should recognise that we protect information and data in similar ways to how we have always looked after our precious things. We lock the doors to our house to keep out unwanted intruders and we password protect our devices. We put childproof locks on cupboards, or safety lids on restrictive chemicals, and we try and restrict a child's access and exposure to certain parts of the internet. We ask our children not to tell someone about a surprise birthday gift, and we are (almost) always surprised when a child too young to understand surprises, or why a birthday has to be on a particular day, spills the secret at the first opportunity. The situation is new, but in many ways, our responses and our understanding are far older.

Nor are these basic principles of safety overly complicated. One of my other projects is a series of storybooks for children called 'Nettie in Cyberland', which introduces the foundations of internet security to children aged 4–6. The project draws on a range of academic work, including Renaud and Prior (2020), which showed that children could be taught about the concept of a password soon after they entered school. These children did not think as adults do and were happy to share their passwords with their school friends and teachers knowing their password, but they drew the line at their siblings! So for many school friends could be trusted but their brother or sister? Knowing *their* password? Absolutely not!

Clearly, then, young children can understand the importance of a password as ensuring separation between their siblings and their secrets, so long as it's explained through a framework, they are familiar with. And, if five-year-olds can, then adults can too.

But how do we make the importance of maintaining this separation between information and the outside world sense to the average employee? And how do we make the processes of separation easy to use and as unobtrusive as possible? The pre-digitalisation equivalent of secure data storage would, for most businesses, have been lockable filing cabinets. While these served the function of preventing those without a key from having access to the data inside, the disruption of needing to keep locking and unlocking the cabinet meant that they were often unlocked in the morning and locked again at night. The risk was seen as being from outsiders such as visitors to the office, or even the cleaners. Even then, before 'clear desk policies' were commonplace, it was often easy enough to find interesting information left out on someone's desk. I've seen this in organisations, too, where a broken photocopier in one location can mean someone accessing another in a secure location and gaining access to all manner of sensitive paperwork on people's desks along the way, either by directly passing their desk or by glancing through the window into their office as I walked past.

From the staff's perspective, tidying and locking away these sensitive documents probably seemed to be an unnecessary hassle as the office was empty on weekends and would require them getting everything back out again on Monday morning anyway. In this case, balancing risk against inconvenience meant taking a risk rather than dealing with the hassle of the secure behaviour. This is a theme we will come back to in Chapter 5 when we look at how the intention to change behaviour can transition into actual behaviour change, and forward into habit. For now, just know that restricting access is almost always going to inconvenience someone, and if that person understands the risks that require that action, then they're far more likely to accept the additional hassle.

So, let's move on to the use of separation for data protection in a workplace working mostly on technical equipment and devices. The use of technology makes it easier to restrict access to information to those with a legitimate need. Pre-COVID, it was quite common to find organisations keeping their sensitive data on a protected shared drive that could only be accessed from within their internal system. Now, this was not foolproof; and there are many situations where such systems have been bypassed, often by benign means like staff forwarding documents to their personal email so they could work on them at home. While this might seem like an easy way to bypass irritating safeguards, the practice still introduces risks around data corruption, loss or leakage during the journey and use at home, all of which can have serious and lasting effects depending on the nature of the information. Indeed, mitigating these risks was one of the biggest challenges associated with the early waves of the pandemic, as many businesses shifted suddenly between office-based and homeworking, with little prior warning or time for preparation.

The result was a massive effort across many sectors of the economy, as infrastructures were renewed or rebuilt for the 'New Normal' that had arrived. Making data securely accessible from outside the office puts greater stress on robust access controls, which determine who does and does not gain access to which files from outside the office. Efficient management of access controls is almost always a challenge, as the processes must account for onboarding new employees; updating permissions to reflect new temporary or permanent positions; or revoking access for employees after they depart. This may seem straightforward in theory, but adding in workplace culture can change everything if, for example, certain staff see having access to different files or projects as a mark of prestige rather than a reflection of their requirement. How, then, do you manage the flow of information? This is, likely, an ongoing problem in many organisations that are starting to review the processes quickly built during the early phases of the pandemic, as restricting access was often not as high a priority as giving access. As hybrid working began to emerge, the requirement to review access bubbled to the surface but needed to be reviewed in a new world with different risks and alongside discussions around the awareness of risk for staff with both those responsible for training and those who are the recipients of the training.

While there are, clearly, many examples of separation as a protection in the physical world, it can be harder to find a technical parallel outside of a work environment but, during a recent Zoom call, a colleague of mine delivered one straight into my lap. A friend of hers works as a childminder, and together they had been discussing children and online safety. The friend then remarked on the difficulties presented by homeschooling, including trusting the children, she was minding with her laptop so that they could do their work. This, apparently, made her very nervous that one of them could accidentally move or delete some of her vital documents such as her work schedule and billing information.

My colleague suggested creating separate user accounts on the laptop for each child which would keep them separate both from her own, personal files and from the files of the other two children she minded. A simple enough solution that took only minutes to put into effect is one that aptly demonstrates how access control in the home can protect data and reduce conflict.

Social Engineering

Social Engineering is one of the most common forms of attack that staff, in their work, and home life, are likely to encounter. But what do we mean when we use the term? According to the Cambridge Dictionary, social engineering is an "*attempt to trick people into giving secret or personal information, especially on the internet, and using it for harmful purposes*", but I would also argue that it can include people being tricked into giving physical access to a place or physical object. Describing this as a form of 'engineering' makes this approach sound systematic and technical which, to be fair, may be in many cases. However, a truly skilled social engineer can nimbly adapt and improvise their approach depending on the reaction of the person they target with ruthless precision – a process which often leaves the victim on the back foot, if they realise what is happening at all.

Social Engineering generally focuses on bridging the protection that comes from separation. This is often discussed in relation to older people, for example, who might find themselves the victims of socially engineered scams that leverage their naivety, or their trust. For example, some people disguise themselves as utility workers and demand payment for fraudulent works that they claim are required. This often ends unhappily for the scam victim. Of course, it's not always the elderly who are tricked; and there are even companies who can be contracted to conduct social engineering 'attacks' on office space in order to test their security protocols. My contacts in such businesses were happy to relay some of the most common tactics they used to gain access to otherwise secure spaces. These included the following:

- Staff are more likely to let you in if it's a wet day, even if the security protocol requires you to wait outside.
- Attractive strangers encounter less resistance and can enter spaces more easily.

- People are more likely to open the door for someone with their hands full. This is even more effective if the strangers' hands are full of food, such as a takeaway order, pizza box, or tray of coffees and confectionery.

These are just a handful of the techniques that can be used against staff who respond from a place of politeness and habit rather than from a place of security. It's even possible that the process of reminding people to be mindful of such intrusions may be more difficult after over a year of hybrid working. As time spent at a formal office will change over the first year or so of 'New Normal working', the familiarity of other people who use the office but may not be close colleagues will be reduced. This is most likely to result in people's reluctance to question someone who is unfamiliar either when they are trying to get into the building or when they are trying to find their way around.

The Door Chain

There are ways of defending against this kind of attack, however. For example, if the concern is that someone with bad intentions might try to force their way into the home of a vulnerable person when they open the door, then this can be countered with the by installation of a good quality door chain to restrict how far the door can open. Homeowners can also ask to inspect a worker's identity card and call the company to verify the authenticity of the visitor. This isn't foolproof either, however, as fake identity cards can come complete with fake numbers to call to verify someone's identity, but here, too, we see the constant war between risk, mitigation and new risk requiring new mitigation.

The important point here is that the door chain is just giving the householder another opportunity to check that the person outside is, in fact, who they say they are. The idea that a person may try and get physical access to your house is something we can all understand. Transposing this into a digital environment, however, introduces new challenges. When should you try to verify if the person on the other end of an email chain is who they say they are? How do you judge who to trust, especially when both legitimate businesses and scam artists can go to great lengths to seem trustworthy and personable?

I once visited a multi-occupancy office building in London. The entrance area was big, and it was very busy. There was a 'bump card' system whereby you had to present your ID card or visitor pass to a scanner before you got to the lift. However, there was another level of security that was almost invisible but very effective: well-trained security personnel, working together as a team. One focused on watching the crowd, and subtly signalled to one of the team when he noticed unusual behaviour, prompting them to step forward and checked the identity of the visitor and, if necessary, checked whether their visit was expected. These staff didn't get in the way of normal activity and were in fact often unnoticed by the regular staff, but they provided another flexible, responsive layer of access control. They were the equivalent of the door chain.

When I am banking online and pay a new person that is deceptively easy. There is no delay, so it appears that there is no 'door chain', no point in holding back the approach. However, in the process of making the payment, two things happened. Firstly, when I put in the payee's account numbers the bank checked that those were legitimate in that they were linked to the person I had named. Then, about an hour after I made that payment, I received a text that told me that a payment had been set up from my account to a new recipient, and giving the time that happened. If that was not me, then I need to go back to my online banking app or phone the bank using the phone number I already have on my bank documents. In the case of the payment being unauthorised, then it will be investigated and the money will be retrieved. In effect, the bank process gives me that door chain protection while the legitimacy of the transaction is checked.

The Confidence Trickster

When I think of a confidence trickster, I have the image in my head from the older version of the 'St. Trinians' films where George Cole plays the sharply dressed, but clearly not entirely law-abiding character 'Flash Harry'. Both his shifty demeanour and his access to goods made it clear that he was not innocent, but he also did no harm to individuals. Tricksters of this type could, supposedly, be spotted easily, making it relatively simple to avoid. As with most things, this can become more difficult to detect in the digital world – not least because you often don't see or even speak directly to the person.

People who use computers for work and leisure don't consider themselves an expert and often feel that they don't understand how to spot or handle an approach from a person who is trying to exploit them.

There is a cartoon, in fact the most well-known cartoon in cybersecurity that was drawn by Peter Steiner for the 'New Yorker' in 1993. It shows a dog standing on an office seat with one paw over the keyboard. The tag line is 'On the Internet nobody knows you're a dog'– and it has a point. Confidence tricksters succeed because, in the absence of meeting the person, we create our own idea of who they are and what they are like. While thinking the best of people is nice, it provides no protection against the world of risks that exist in digital space.

Example One – Kitchen Composter

This is a real example, and yes, I am the victim who nearly lost money in this scam. This happened in the COVID summer when the weather was good enough that it was possible to do some work in the garden after the end of the working day. Sometime later, I saw an advert for device that sits in the kitchen and composts your food waste into fertiliser for the garden. This sounded great to me and for £29.99 it was not cheap, but not a huge risk, I bought one. I had to wait a while, but transport of goods across the world was slow at that point so I didn't worry. Then I got notification that my parcel would be delivered that day. How exciting.

Imagine my shock and disappointment when my composter turned out to be a bag of bin bags.

I then went onto the internet to try and find the composter on another site. I finally found the actual unit on the manufacturer's website at the more realistic cost of $545 Canadian.

I had been scammed. Fortunately, I had used PayPal to pay and, after a bit of hassle from the seller, I got my money back. Lesson learnt. A few weeks later I saw another item for sale on the same social media platform and this time I did a bit of investigation and again something that was for sale at £27.50 cost over £300 on other sites – and no I didn't buy it this time.

Several years ago, I commissioned this image to encourage people to think about the person who is trying to defraud them online in the same way they would if they were confronted by the person physically. Even now I find this one illustration turns

around perception and allows people to see scams for what they really are – a way of trying to rob you using technology.

Example Two – Grooming

One of the worst things about falling for a scam or online fraud is that it is far too easy to place the blame on the victim rather than the perpetrator. After all, if only they had stopped to think about it even for a moment, then common sense would have told them that they were being tricked! This is, however, short-sighted at best and cruel at worst. Confidence tricksters ply their trade by being clever, charismatic and manipulative, leading to situations where the victim doesn't know how much danger they are in until they are deep within the web of deception.

Think of the time we have just lived through where lockdown meant that some people were very isolated for a long time. Now consider a situation where an attacker played to that weakness and sought to attract someone into an email conversation. It would be like having a 'pen pal', someone whose email you were looking forward to because they seemed to be so nice. It would not take long before a small request for a bit of financial help would seem reasonable. For example, they tell their correspondent that their car has broken down and it is three weeks until they get paid, and they need the car to get to work. Could they just borrow £40 to pay for the new car part? Just like an angler they don't pull too hard at first. Just put out a bit of bait and see if the victim is willing to help, with the requests scaling up over time in such a way that each step itself might seem small, and that can make it difficult to escape the trap once within it. On the outside, it is easy to mock those who have fallen for such an approach, but realistically most of us are vulnerable given the right circumstances and approach.

Situational Awareness

As IT equipment has become more common in the workplace, the focus for safety and security has increasingly shifted to almost exclusively IT equipment and even messages about secure behaviour tend to be around a directly technical threat, such as not opening phishing emails. According to these warnings, we _become_ the breach when we click on a bad link within the email and we become the flaw in the technical defence. However, I recently heard a great point on this subject. They said that a good technical defence will block or reject such approaches. Only when the technology has _failed_ do the humans become critical to defence. It is also worth remembering, however, that there are more threats than suspicious links and suspect emails. The security around how we behave with our devices, where we sit, the use of passwords, or leaving a phone unguarded when we go to a counter to collect our food or drink are less common as a security focuses.

I enjoy travelling on trains for work, and I find that especially where I am able to work in the business section of the train, there are often some fascinating discussions that go on between colleagues on their way to, or from, meetings with clients. The people involved are generally so focused on their discussion, that they don't think about themselves in the environment, or who else might be sitting within earshot, or what they might get from the information being broadcast so publicly.

Ira Winkler, an information security specialist for many years, said,

There's something about the device that causes people to relax and let their guards down.

'Information Security is Security'

(1998)

And I couldn't agree more, although I would stretch the statement to cover more technical interactions. For example, there has long been a concern that accidents were being caused by people driving and using their mobile phones. It wasn't just about the fact they were holding the phone in their hand, although obviously if one hand is navigating around the phone it is not available to help to steer the car, but that is also true for someone eating while driving. It is the splitting of cognitive focus between what is going on around the car and what is on the phone screen, this means that the driver's situational awareness is significantly reduced. It is not just mobile phones that do this: answering a call, while contending with inconsistent WiFi on the train, and keeping an eye out for the next stop can easily consume much of the mental 'space' necessary for, for example, keeping a track on which customer names you do, or don't mention, or how loud your voice might be.

Cognitive Bandwidth

This term describes the fact that most people have a limited number of things they can be concentrating on at one time. This is not the same as situational awareness as it comes from the activity the person is involved in. When we come to people who work in a public space they must try and concentrate on the work they are doing, and that can be challenging. When they become absorbed, they are using most of their mental capacity, or more correctly their cognitive bandwidth on their task and are therefore much less likely to see that someone sitting close who is shoulder surfing their work or paying close attention to a phone call they are having.

An example of this was given to me by a colleague who was travelling on a train for work. During their journey, one of the other passengers was business setting up the lease of a flat for their son who was going to Edinburgh as a student. This involved not only setting up the lease for which he was to be the guarantor but also setting up the monthly direct debit to ensure the rent was paid. This meant that a wide range of personal details were required by the letting agents including name, date of birth, home address and bank details of the passenger, and the personal information about his son as well. As my colleague was bored, he took note of all the sensitive information that was shared with everyone in the carriage. When the call was over, he went across to the passenger and gave him the piece of paper with all the information on it, and his business card that showed he was the head of information security at a major financial institution. Needless to say, the passenger was amazed and horrified by the sheer amount of information he had shared without a second thought. Because his cognitive focus was on getting the flat organised, he paid no attention to what he was saying and any who could overhear. The passenger was very grateful for the warning, one can only hope that he went back to work and not only was more aware of his own insecurity but also shared the story with other colleagues and let them learn from his mistake.

Unfortunately, it is simply not feasible to roam public spaces across the country looking for opportunities to educate people about the need for information security, or how easily they might lose control of their data. Maybe organisations need to consider the risks involved in this workspace to be worthy of a targeted educational campaign.

3

THE CHALLENGES OF COMMUNICATING ABOUT SECURITY AWARENESS

Introduction

One of the positive and negative points about security awareness is that, if it can be well devised and targeted, then a change of process or behaviour can seem like common sense, in that it is an obviously safer way to work. To believe that security awareness is all like that is to misunderstand the risks, threats and impacts on normal working practices – impacts that can mean that they are not as warmly received. In reality, there is, at most a 'sweet spot' at which the information is received and implemented without a backward glance to the 'pre-change' situation.

A range of elements including cultural context in the organisation and even across different groups in an organisation can make a difference to which approach is most successful. As someone pointed out to me recently, people working in a call centre will not generally have the time or inclination to read an article on awareness, while other staff may feel that the use of cartoon images seems trivial. Add those challenges to the impact of most staff working in physical separation from their colleagues, and it becomes a lot more than 'common sense'.

So why is it so difficult to convince people to become (in)security-aware and behave appropriately, when the basic concepts and preventative steps are familiar to us? I like to refer clients to the four R's:

- **Resistance**: *This is all common sense, training is a waste of my time*
- **Reluctance**: *I don't want to engage with this, training takes time I could be using for other things*
- **Relevance**: *Why should I go to this training, it isn't relevant to me*
- **Revision**: *I've already had this training, so why should I go again?*

DOI: 10.1201/9781003194583-4

33

Resistance

It is almost a cliché to say that people tend to resist change – but it's true! Having an established, familiar way of doing things allows us to shift into autopilot, reducing our mental load. Over time, these patterns become so ingrained that the idea of changing our behaviour can feel overwhelming, especially when we are living through times of unprecedented stress and disruption.

As with most issues of information security, the challenges we're facing here are not entirely new. Look at the disruption that occurred when organisations realised that they needed to manage and dispose of paper documentation in a secure way as an example. This change in practice caused significant disruption as waste disposal became more complicated, with staff now needing to make decisions about whether each document they disposed of contained sensitive information and then act appropriately. This might not seem like a significant issue, as the difference between disposing of documents securely might only mean crossing the office to dispose of their documents in a specified location, rather than using the bin at their desk. Such an inconvenience seems like a small price to pay for preventing potential data breach or data loss – but even this disruption can lead to protocols being underused or disregarded entirely.

Being active in the information security community at this time meant that I often found myself in conversations around just this kind of issue. I heard many tales of senior information security professionals suspecting a failure of protocol, and easily proving their suspicions correct by walking through the office in the evening and pulling documents containing sensitive information out of desk-side bins before they had been emptied.

But what was the solution? Certainly not the carefully crafted email that was sent to remind employees of the correct procedure. Even installing more secure bins throughout the office, to decrease the time and disruption of following the correct procedure produced only limited results. Finally, the information security team took a different approach. They opened up secure disposal to allow staff to dispose of their own private documents, as well as their work-related paperwork. The results were slow at first, but after six weeks there were significantly fewer sensitive documents being disposed of incorrectly.

Why did this work? The answer is simple enough: disposing of documents securely suddenly had personal, as well as professional, benefits. Opening secure disposal to all documents, whether work related or not, started to answer the quiet "why" question lurking in the back of the minds of staff. Why should they dispose of sensitive documents securely? Because they were *their* documents, holding *their* information, and once sorting sensitive documents became a habit, there was less resistance when making those same decisions in the office – because now this new disposal system was simply *the way it was done*.

This is one of the reasons I always emphasise the importance of explaining the 'why' behind a particular protocol, as well as the 'what'. Not because staff will necessarily challenge the policy outright or even realise the source of their own resistance but because we know the difficulties it can cause, and how much easier it is to deal with it at the outset, than retrain and remediate at a later stage. Not only that but teaching your staff to think critically about different policies is an important step towards being insecurity-aware! Teaching staff that they should ask questions about new procedures and question both the 'why' and the 'how' helps to create an environment where information security becomes a goal that we work towards together, rather than just being seen as the role of the information security manager and their team.

This brings us to another moment when resistance might arise – when your staff understand the necessary procedure, the reasons behind it, but see that the rules are being applied inconsistently. For example, consider the relatively common policy of saying that company computers should not be taken outside the country. In this case, the rule might be inconvenient if, for example, the staff member is required to attend events or conferences that are held internationally as it can make it difficult to work during the event or edit the planned presentation once at the destination.

Consider the impact that going through this stressful process might have, if you then see other senior people in your company doing *exactly* what you have been told not to do, without repercussions. I've certainly been in positions like this and felt that same resistance to following the rules when attending the next international event, as I'm now being 'penalised' (with inconvenience) for following the rules, while others ignore that rule with no issue at all. Contrast this with how it would feel to see senior people at the company following the same rules, dealing with the same impact on workflow and inconvenience, and prioritising information security anyway. Now there is no conflict, but a role model in a senior position demonstrating secure practices, further reinforcing the culture of security in the organisation with the silent message that *this is how we do things here.*

One of my favourite examples of the power that senior management can have as role models comes from Thomas Watson Jr., who was the president of IBM from 1952 to 1971.

On this particular day, Mr. Watson was touring the production plant with his entourage. The security procedure was relatively simple with coloured ID badges indicating which areas particular people should, or should not, have access to. In this case, orange badges granted access to most areas of the plant, with particularly sensitive areas requiring an additional green badge for access.

The story goes that Watson and his colleagues approached one of these more sensitive areas and were greeted by a security officer, as procedure dictated. What the procedure did *not* allow for was what should happen if the president of the company himself remembers his orange pass for general access but forgets his green pass for entry into more secure areas.

Here the security officer had two choices: allow Mr. Watson to enter despite lacking the proper card, on the basis that she not only knew him but his position and the clearance it provided, or insist that the proper procedure was followed. Tension mounted as the security officer made it clear that she was bound by the procedure and could not permit the company president into the secure area without the proper ID badge. It was a bold decision, and one that might have cost the security officer her job, if Watson had not agreed and sent one of his entourage back to his office to collect his green badge, only continuing once he, too, had the proper clearance on display.

Stories like these can travel at lightning speed through an organisation. Imagine the impact of knowing that no one, not even the president of the company, is above following the security procedure even when time is precious or when following the procedure is inconvenient. That's a powerful message – and all it costs was a few minutes of extra time.

Security procedures like these are not alien to us now. In fact, they've become a part of our daily lives, whether we're at work or not, as we navigate whether facemasks are recommended or required, and in what situation. The introductions of these policies have been met with a tide of questions, many of them hinging on this critical 'why', and in some cases, 'why should *I* when *they* do not?', which perhaps provides a better example of what can happen if procedures are seen as being inconsistently communicated and followed than any scenario I could create for this book.

We will doubtlessly meet more of this resistance as we emerge into 'The New Normal era', whether it's in the context of negotiating working in the office versus hybrid working versus working from home, or in the context of general life itself. And while it is not our role to influence how staff might follow procedure in their private lives, we should be sensitive to how they are responding to changing procedures and regulations in general as we introduce our own. Certainly, we should expect to see far more overt questioning of 'why' than we have before, as people find themselves living through the later stages of the pandemic, and the long recovery period to follow – which will bring its own stresses.

We need to think about this context as we shift the focus towards insecurity awareness and be sensitive to the challenges of learning new patterns of behaviour for working from home, when previous habits (such as locking the computer screen when stepping away from the desk at work) had become unthinking habit. Introducing similar procedures into homeworking, where people might not see the 'why', can lead to resistance as they doubt how necessary these inconvenient procedures really are. Add to this the potential for those old, reflexive habits to have faded over the course of the pandemic, making them once again feel inconvenient when people return to the office, and we should all prepare for a bumpy ride.

Reluctance

The difference between resistance and reluctance is the energy behind it.

You are *reluctant* to get out of bed in the morning; you will *resist* someone dumping you in an icy shower to wake you up. And while it may seem counter-intuitive, overcoming this reluctance and apathy can often be more challenging than addressing direct resistance in many cases! After all, active resistance has some energy being it – and that energy can be redirected – whereas reluctance does not. Overcoming reluctance requires not only addressing the 'why' problem but doing so in a way that breaks the apathy, motivating them to embrace the new procedure.

Let's take the example of visibility screens for mobile devices. When I mentioned my own research earlier, I described how easy it could be for people to 'shoulder surf', to see and even capture pictures of information that was accessed in public. This is one of my biggest concerns as an information security professional, because while it might take a minute of squinting and straining to read someone's screen while on the train, it takes seconds to pull out a phone, with an increasingly high-resolution camera, and capture that data to read at some later time. Given the risk involved in such exposure, it would seem like visibility screens, which restrict the angle and distance from which a screen can be viewed, are an easy and relatively low-cost solution – so why do we not see them more often in general use?

I found some of the clearest answers to this question, not in the academic literature, but in the review sections of websites like Amazon. Here we can see the (relatively) unfiltered experience of the user, and here I found the minor but consistent reasons for not using this kind of safety equipment: dust and difficulty fitting the screens to the devices in a way that did not hinder the use of the device itself. It's important to realise that complaints like these don't indicate resistance – users were not pushing back against the introduction of the screens themselves – rather they found them inconvenient and did not see the benefit of putting up with these practical issues without any obvious benefit.

Now in an ideal world, we would have the opportunity to follow up on comments like these, to ask why they had originally purchased the screen in the first place, what they believed the dangers were and why that didn't balance against the inconvenience of the screen itself. Obviously, this isn't possible for Amazon reviews – but it is, perhaps, worth considering if you find yourself meeting similar resistance from others when it comes to taking simple steps to enhance data security.

It is important to remember several things when we have these kinds of conversations, however. Firstly, we are not responding to active resistance, so we're not working with people who have a direct, negative opinion of the procedure we're introducing. They're not just against change as a default, they're just more comfortable doing things 'the way they've always done them', because familiarity becomes habit, and habits are far easier to follow than they are to break. From this perspective, it makes sense that people will be reluctant to take on new security practices when it means giving up the way they have been working before. Remember, many of these well-worn behaviours will have been developed and adapted over time, and stress-tested in busy environments so that they make day-to-day life easier.

One of the least helpful solutions to reluctance that I've come across is a security professional who came to me during a professional net-working event. I was talking with a group of people who I had not met before and asked, as a bit of an 'ice breaker', I asked how people made sure that their staff locked their screens when stepping away from their computer. There were a range of answers, including reminders that appeared when the computer started in the morning and posters hung in eye-catching places – but the answer that brought the con-versation to an abrupt halt was one professional who answered confi-dently that his staff locked their screens "because they will get sacked if they don't".

After a moment of trying to determine if the professional was jok-ing, discussion turned to whether this was, in fact, an appropriate practice, with one of the group members suggesting he check with his HR department about how this kind of sanction lined up with the employment contracts of the staff he was threatening to fire. Perhaps, we suggested, he might want to follow that conversation with one with an employment lawyer, who would likely agree with the HR representative when they likely informed this manager that failing to lock your computer screen was not a dismissible offence.

For this reason, it is important to distinguish between deliberate action in the form of resistance and non-compliance in the form of reluctance. Those who actively push against a screen-locking policy need a different approach than those who remember to lock their screen if the office is busy, or when they are going away for a long period, but forget if the office is emptier, or they're only expecting to be away for a minute or two. And we have to crack this difference because adopting a hybrid model of working will mean that offices are, in general, less crowded, leading to more insecure practices if we're dealing with the second case rather than the first. These employees will respond to different techniques than those who are actively resisting a policy, and should be supported to comply, rather than punished for their perceived resistance.

It's not just about how we communicate our procedures when we're communicating directly with people, either. I once reviewed a Cyber Incident Response Plan and found that the writer had concluded a paragraph describing different ways of reporting a cybersecurity incident with a sentence that said "failure to report a cyber incident will result in disciplinary action being taken". This threat of severe action only undermined the paragraph of helpfully phrased text above it, as it took the focus away from empowering the staff member to be insecurity-aware and respond appropriately and replaced it with a threat of reprisal if they were perceived to have failed in the reporting process.

Thankfully, these are issues that are easy to fix, and usually come from multiple people working on the same document from different perspectives at different times. After some discussion, we simply replaced the sentence with one that reinforced the organisations 'no blame' policy and encouraged the reader to report the incident no matter the situation. This meant that staff who, in a moment of poor judgement, opened a suspicious email, file or link would be more likely to report the mistake promptly rather than attempting to hide their mistake out of fear. This, in turn, would allow the security team to respond quickly and effectively for any potential breach, rather than waiting until it was uncovered, or worse, until the system was clearly and catastrophically compromised. This doesn't mean that inappropriate or insecure behaviour shouldn't be addressed as a matter of course, but that policies need to be designed carefully to ensure that they uphold a standard of behaviour, while encouraging reporting.

Relevance

One of the easiest 'why' questions to overlook is this: "why is this relevant *to me?*", often leading our information security strategies to suffer as a result. Identifying exactly what each person needs to know, for what reason, and when, can be drawn out and is a frustrating process, and that's before we consider how we should communicate that information to the target audience.

Designing high-quality training around information security requires walking this line over, and over, and over again – knowing that the training will have to be adapted slightly each time as you learn more about what works for specific audiences, but this process is a key step in building insecurity awareness in your organisation. As a professional trainer, I know how easy it is to fall into a pattern of delivering things in a similar way every time, but we should resist this urge as much as we can. Information security training must be tailored to its audience and that means considering not only the information you're trying to get across but the people you're trying to get it across to.

It's vital that we remember we are not our audience, and our audience are not us.

The staff we train may not share our understanding of information security risks, or how the processes and technologies we use protect the organisation from digital threats – yet it's all too easy for us to forget that we're not all starting from the same 'page' when we deliver training. It's easier to remember that staff in different positions will have different levels of understanding of the organisation's procedures than it is to remember that there can be a huge difference in knowledge within staff teams at the same level. Each person will come to their role with a different level of experience of using different pieces of technology – and we should always be mindful of this, meet our audience at their skill level and work from there.

I think Donald Rumsfeld summed this up best when he said,

> *As we know, there are known knowns; there are things we know we know.*
> *We also know there are known unknowns; that is to say, we know there are some things we do not know.*
> *But there are also unknown unknowns – the ones we don't know we don't know.*
> 12th February 2002

So, in terms of security awareness, there are things we know that staff know and understand, such as leaving your company laptop on the train could lead to a data leak and a very uncomfortable discussion with your line manager. These known knowns should still be refreshed and reminded from time to time – ideally through a system of subtle 'nudges'. Nudges are quick reminders to take particular action or do things in a particular way. Tim Ward of 'Think Cyber Security' gives more detail on the four components of an effective nudge, saying they should be:

- Easy – This is just reminding the user of something they already know so the message can be simple.
- Attractive – A nudge must grab the attention of users or is an attractive activity.
- Social – This identifies the activity as one that most of their colleagues are doing, so it can be identified as a behaviour norm.
- Timely – The nudge must be delivered immediately before user engages in the task.

It's vital that we think carefully about how we can support staff to behave more securely as we develop our information security plans, and the insecurity awareness of our staff in this new post-COVID era. We need to build a thorough understanding of what they know and what they don't – where they need nudges, where they need training and where they might be meeting new procedures with reluctance or resistance. It's only by understanding all of these factors that we can design effective strategies for data security that function in the flexible and shifting landscape of blended working and shifting restrictions.

Revision

So, if we manage 'known knowns' through nudges, how do we prepare for the unknowns? This is the challenge. The world of work has changed and will continue to adjust over the next three or four years as work patterns evolve to suit this 'New Normal' we have found ourselves in. Yet, even the most effective security manager will not be able to predict and protect against all avenues of possible attack all of the time.

It is important that we remember, and remind our staff, that cyber threats, like viruses, will mutate and evolve to find vulnerabilities, often faster than we expect. This changing landscape of cyber risks is why we need to encourage staff to become insecurity-aware, such that a user becomes suspicious when they encounter something unexpected and take action to raise awareness of it. This is where developing a two-way communication between those who have formal responsibility for cybersecurity and the end users is so important. We need to create systems that make it as easy to reach out when staff encounter something suspicious while working from home as it is when we are physically present together in a traditional office. Encouraging staff to raise even small or 'silly' concerns will help to strengthen their information insecurity 'muscles' over time, making them an increasingly effective protective element over time.

This process can, and should, then be followed up with targeted training that revises key information security practices in the light of new, or developing, risks. This process will feel drastically different when working with audiences who understand their role in the information security process compared to those who don't. Staff who have been supported to understand the 'whys' behind procedures, as well as the 'what' of what they are asked to do, will be more likely to engage with updated content and new threats – because they are invested in the process.

We know this to be true, too – we've seen it over the course of the pandemic. Think carefully about how many people you know have talked about the challenges of making sure that sensitive phone calls were not overheard by others when working from home. If your first instinct was to say none, I invite you to think again and look for the small steps taken to make sure that couples could work from home at the same time without constantly being heard in each other's meetings, or by their child's teacher while they were learning remotely. These steps might seem minor, but they're evidence of a consistent level of awareness that works to our advantage as we train and support staff to become insecurity-aware. We don't have to convince people that they have to work securely from home in principle, we need to show them the 'whens', 'hows' and whys of the practical actions they need to take and build from there.

The only thing we can guarantee is that there will be new challenges in the years to come and that there will always be a need to alert staff to new risks and their impact. Procedures will always need to be updated, and we will all need to adapt our behaviour in light of them – but we do not need to do this work in isolation. Instead, we can work with staff across the organisation to create a strong, multi-faceted protective shield around the organisation and its data that will be more effective than any single security awareness communication could ever be.

4

TAKING ON AN INVISIBLE THREAT

An Exercise in Understanding and Defending Against Data Leakage

Introduction

One of the biggest challenges we will face as information security professionals in a world of increasingly blended and flexible working is invisible data loss. We've touched on this briefly in previous chapters, but we will talk about it in more detail now – starting with perhaps the most important question: how common is invisible data loss?

The answer to this is complicated and leans heavily on the work that myself and other colleagues in the information security sector have been doing over the last 10–15 years, but the premise is simple enough. Invisible data loss can occur when people gain access to information that they shouldn't simply by being in proximity to the person who is using that data.

This is more common than you might think, because of the challenges of working in a data-rich environment is easy to forget that documents which are familiar or dull to us may still be interesting or eye-catching to someone in our environment. In fact, it's possible, and even likely, that you've captured data this way yourself! My favourite example of this came from a friend of mine who used to travel between major cities by train on a regular basis. Now, it wasn't (and isn't) uncommon for people to work while on the train, but on this occasion, she found herself sitting next to a solicitor who was working on a particular case. My friend knew this not because she was acquainted with the solicitor in question but because they had several documents spread across their shared table, giving her visual access to the documents, and she recognised the case from the local headlines that had been published at the time the person involved was arrested. Now, my friend claims to have rallied her self-control and resisted

DOI: 10.1201/9781003194583-5

reading the documents – but I don't know if I would have had the same discipline if I was in her situation!

This process, whereby someone's attention is caught by the documents on our table, or the documents on our screen, and then accessed either by being read at the moment or by being captured on camera for later review, is called shoulder surfing. Shoulder surfing itself isn't a new problem, but it represents a more significant threat as we move further into a modern world where huge numbers of documents might be accessed while in public spaces, surrounded by people with increasingly powerful cameras on their personal devices and easy access to online spaces where images can be shared easily.

My own journey of investigating and raising awareness of shoulder surfing began in what seems like a most unlikely location – an Information Security Conference in 2008. It was here that I noticed that people were happy to speak freely about their experiences during questions and networking events, which might not have seemed odd if it were not for the large professional camera that was regularly moving around the area throughout the day to capture video of the conference and its attendees. You might think that a room full of information security professionals might become uncomfortable or change topic as the camera approached – but they didn't. Instead, the camera, and

its operator, faded into the background, despite being anything but subtle – as the following picture shows!

I found this security blind spot so fascinating that I tracked down E Eugene Schultz, commonly considered as one of the founding fathers of modern information security, what could be causing people who spent their days thinking and practicing information security to ignore such an obvious data capture device. Gene thought about this for some time before telling me that that was a very interesting question that I should go and find the answer to! Sadly, we lost Gene before I could complete my Master's research on the topic – but I think he would be proud of what we've learned.

It's important to realise that this event provided an example of two types of data leakage, oral (or spoken) data that was picked up by the microphone and visual data captured by the camera. This provided the cameraman or anyone with access to the footage the opportunity to access data by 'overlistening' (where someone makes an active choice to listen in on a conversation, rather than 'overhearing' which implies passively being aware of a nearby conversation without any effort to listen in), as well as shoulder surfing and viewing the information captured on video.

I've noticed that discussing these concepts at conferences and during training sessions tends to get a similar set of results every time. There will, for example, usually be those who were either unaware of the problem or do not recognise it as a potential security threat. Others will go quiet, as they think about the idea – often with increasingly worried expressions as I imagine they replay in their head all of the times they've worked on sensitive documents in public, in cafes and airport lounges and so on. And then there are those who immediately resonate with the idea and are keen to share their experiences – like a colleague of mine who immediately described sitting on a train with someone who was attempting to book a weekend break. Over the course of the train ride, he told me, he heard not only when the break would be, but the name of the people taking the trip, their full home address and their credit card details. As a result, he ended the trip not only with enough information to misuse their credit card details but their home address and when their house would be left empty. This was a major security breach of their personal details and they had no idea until he approached to warn them about exactly what he had heard.

To say they were not pleased was an understatement. In fact, the passenger was offended that he had the audacity to listen to the private calls – placing the blame on him, rather than accepting the responsibility of protecting their data as their own. This response is understandable, especially at the moment, but demonstrates a lack of understanding of the potential risks of accessing or relaying sensitive data in shared spaces. As a result, the passenger's only defence against fraud was the moral standing of her fellow passengers, which any risk manager would recognise as an exceptionally weak safeguard against such significant risk.

In the name of practicing what I preach, I worked alongside an artist to illustrate this phenomenon, which I describe as a 'Virtual Booth', to help non-security professionals relate more easily to the concept.

Here, you can see what we have described in the last two pages of text, demonstrated in a single image. In the centre position, the worker sits surrounded in a vague haze of presumed privacy – no one, they think, will enter that space and yet the waiter on the left is able to shoulder surf the data on his screen with ease, while the customer on the right deliberately overlistens to his phone call. It's easy to slip into our virtual booth and forget our surroundings, especially when we are focused on something difficult or detailed, but we (and our staff!) must always remember that the booth is ultimately a lie we tell

ourselves, built on an automatic trust in others to act in our best inter-est. It is perhaps the ultimate example of insecurity *un*awareness.

Yet as with most information security risks this issue isn't entirely new either. There have been many studies demonstrating how easy it can be to miss even the most eye-catching events when our focus is directed elsewhere. One of my favourite light-hearted examples of this is an experiment by Hyman [insert reference] who investigated the impact of using a (then cutting edge) smartphone on people's situ-ational awareness by interviewing students as they exited a particu-lar university courtyard. A courtyard that had contained a unicycling clown – a fact which students who had been looking at their phones often missed, despite its absolute absurdity!

These experiments were more than an excuse to make use of the obscure talents of junior researchers, however. Over time experiments like these were laid alongside real-world data to show the potential dangers of trying to use a smartphone while focusing on other tasks, like driving. The issue itself comes from our own limited cognitive bandwidth, which essentially limits how many things we can focus on at any time, forcing our brain to direct our mental processing power towards the tasks we're trying to focus on while allowing other factors to fall out of our attention. The depth of this focus can then be influ-enced by our cognitive involvement – or how deeply we are immersed in the task – and external pressures such as deadlines that push us to focus more tightly on the task at hand.

An Invisible Issue

By now, you might be wondering where the problem is. Surely, if so many people are able to recognise and resonate with examples of being exposed to other people's data in a variety of situations, then it should be easy to demonstrate the risk and convince individuals to take the steps necessary to mitigate it in the future.

Or perhaps you've seen one of the big issues around protect-ing against this kind of data breach – how do you *prove* there is a problem?

This is where practices like shoulder surfing become difficult to challenge, because unlike lost disks, stolen laptops or catastrophic sys-tem hacks, capturing information this way doesn't leave a trace. How do you motivate a workforce to protect against a risk you can't clearly point at and prove exists?

My approach was to demonstrate the *potential* for data to be compromised in this way, rather than waiting until I could show evidence of a potentially catastrophic data leak. After all, the question is no longer 'how much would another person remember of what they have seen' but 'how much data can they capture without being detected'.

The White Hole Model

While I was working on this problem of demonstrating the risk of shoulder surfing, my husband was taking an interest in astronomy. This led to many conversations on a variety of topics about which I knew very little and he knew quite a bit, and while I've forgotten many of the details in the time since one concept stuck with me. The idea struck me as we were talking over dinner one evening, and he began to explain how scientists could detect a black hole. Black holes, he said, couldn't be directly captured with our current imaging technology, meaning that scientists discovered and researched these almost-invisible phenomena by watching the way that things moved into them or around them.

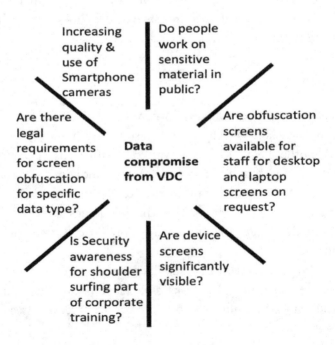

Increasing quality & use of Smartphone cameras

Do people work on sensitive material in public?

Are there legal requirements for screen obfuscation for specific data type?

Data compromise from VDC

Are obfuscation screens available for staff for desktop and laptop screens on request?

Is Security awareness for shoulder surfing part of corporate training?

Are device screens significantly visible?

Well, I thought. If that's not as good a starting point as any, I don't know what is. And so the 'White Hole Model' was born. As you can see, this model begins to demonstrate the potential of data loss via shoulder surfing (Visual Data Capture or VDC for short) by examining the factors that would surround that kind of data capture.

Do people work on sensitive material in public? This was perhaps one of the easiest factors to demonstrate, as I simply asked a number of volunteers to keep a record of the kind of information they were able to shoulder surf while carrying out their daily activities. The results came in thick and fast, and it quickly became clear that the answer to this question was a resounding 'yes'. In fact, it has been a yes ever since, as even mentioning method in training or during presentations tends to lead to a number of follow-up conversations with people eager to tell me about the weird and interesting data they've seen in public spaces.

Are device screens significantly visible? The next step was to test how close an observer would need to be to capture a useable image displayed on a tablet device. The answer, even in as far back as 2015, was not nearly as close as you might think. To test this, I set up a 'user' with a tablet device at a shared table and explored what data could be captured by those sitting in line with them on either side, as well as by those one and two rows back. I used the same layout in 2015 and again in 2017 to explore the impact of changing technologies, including more convenient tablet devices and more powerful integrated phone cameras. Each time onlookers were able to capture the entire screen with ease, at a level of detail that left the text legible and able to be read again in the future.

Is security awareness for shoulder surfing part of corporate training? Interestingly, the answer to this appeared to be both yes and no. On one hand, most people reported that they had never been given any specific training or advice about shoulder surfing as part of their training. On the other hand, most workplaces did have policies in place that limited visual access to data in some way – usually in the form of forcing staff to lock their screen when leaving their desk and so on. Some businesses even required their staff to use obfuscation screens as a matter of course – which protects against this risk. This suggests that the foundations have been laid for this kind of awareness, and we need to take the next step.

Are there legal requirements for screen obfuscation for specific data types? While not widespread, there are already particular pieces

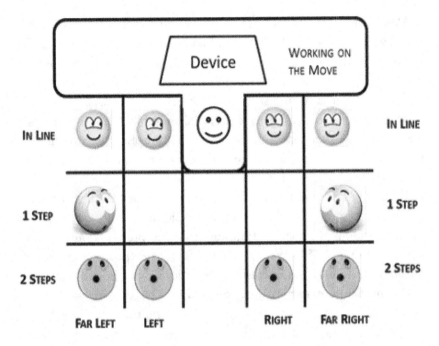

of legislation that require screens to be protected from unauthorised visual access and visual data capture. The Health Insurance Portability and Accountability Act (HIPAA) 1996 and Health Information Technology for Economic and Clinical Health Act (HITECH) were key drivers in developing obfuscation software and screens, for example. Nor is it unusual to find offices in the UK and beyond introducing these measures within an office space, especially where workers are dealing with sensitive financial or personal information.

The presence of these factors, alongside other indicators, demonstrates that not only is there an increased risk of data loss via shoulder surfing and visual data capture but that there is a corporate and legal will to mitigate these risks where people become aware of them. Making people aware of and sensitive to this risk, then, is the next challenge.

Raising Awareness Around Visual Data Loss

I have always found it helpful to work through key images, rather than relying on text alone when providing security awareness training – so let's work through the following model.

Working in Public

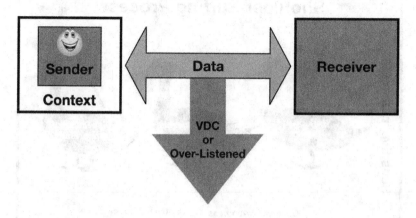

Starting at the top left, the observed person (and 'sender' of information) is working in a public place. For now, we don't need to discuss *why* this person feels like they could, should or must access sensitive data in a secure location, but I strongly recommend facilitating that conversation as part of any training you provide as doing so will help you understand how staff are making decision around balancing the risk of working in public with the reward of doing so.

As we move from the observed person, who is not aware of what is going on because they are in their 'virtual booth' of focus, we can see the intended path that the data *should* travel – from the sender to the receiver. While the information arrives at its intended receiver uninterrupted, some of that data is also 'captured' by the unseen observer who might be shoulder surfing or overlistening while the sender completes their task. And because this leak happens without interrupting the transfer, between sender and receiver, and so often goes unnoticed.

Sharing Data

So now some of the data have been shared with an unauthorised person, who may have even captured or recorded it for later review. Now the risk shifts from if the data is captured to how it might be used. In many situations, it will be forgotten or shared only as a story between family, friends or at information security events. Often this is where the leak ends, as the people told have no reason to remember the information, but not always.

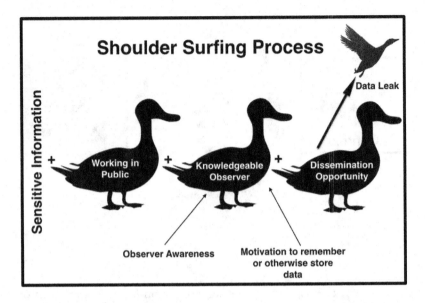

Sometimes the opposite will happen, and the situation will line up like ducks in a row, resulting in substantial data leaks and significant damage to the organisation.

Sensitive Information

While the information that two people are discussing may be interesting or entertaining, it is not necessarily sensitive information in a business sense. If this situation occurs with sensitive information, then the risk comes from the unseen observer being someone with enough knowledge to recognise the value of the information and the ability to benefit from its capture. From there, the risk becomes what the observer does with that information, and how serious the results of those actions are. This is the last unknown in the sequence, as technological advances make it easier and easier to share detailed information or images quickly, whether that's by selling it directly to a newspaper eager to fill their 24-hour news cycle.

A Security Awareness Lesson

So how do we teach staff to be more aware of a threat that is so difficult to detect at the moment? It turns out the answer might be easier

Awareness Re-Enforcement Loop

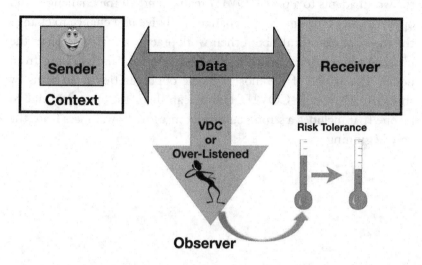

than we think – it just needs us to think outside the box. Information Security Awareness training usually begins by educating someone about a risk, showing how their behaviour creates vulnerability, before finally introducing the new behaviour of system that manages the risk in question. For shoulder surfing, it helps to begin the process by encouraging people to notice the risk for themselves.

I found that volunteers in my research often reported that keeping watch for examples of other people working insecurely in public places made them more aware of their own working practices. Importantly, this increased over time, as watching for insecure situations became a habit, which in turn increased their own perception of the risk of working in public places and lowered their tolerance to it. I describe this as an Awareness Re-Enforcement Loop, where the person's experience of being the Observer directly impacts their behaviour when they are in the role of the Sender and so on.

Resisting an Invisible Threat

While the concept of invisible data loss via shoulder surfing, visual data capture or overlistening may seem small in the context of some of the software-based risks we manage as part of Information Security Management, it's vital we address it as part of our management plans.

The next few years will see constant shifts in working practices as the world adapts to a post-COVID reality, and all the challenges and opportunities it brings. These changes will give us a chance to change the way that staff think about their work practices as they re-enter the physical office after years of COVID restrictions and working from home. This is one of the most valuable opportunities given to us by this shift into a 'post-COVID' era: we can shape the 'New Normal' to be one that includes a strong culture of insecurity awareness from the very beginning.

5

TURNING 'BEHAVIOURAL INTENT' INTO HABITUAL BEHAVIOUR

Introduction

In the period after we set resolutions for the New Year, often well thought out and generally intended, gyms and those in the 'slimming profession' know that this is going to be a peak for them. They know that this is when gym memberships are signed and diets are subscribed to. They also know that by the time the spring brings the return of colour to our environment, many will have left their daily exercising routines or weekly fasting way behind.

When you consider that these targets are set, most believe that they will get personal benefit from changing their behaviour. When we are trying to change the way that people work in order to protect data more effectively, we don't have that same personal motivation. Of course, people can be threatened, but given, as we said in the previous chapter, leaks are often invisible, and even then, it is probably untraceable. How then can we make those behavioural changes stick?

In the last chapter, I used the example of 'shoulder surfing' to show the challenges of making people aware of risks that they may not have recognised before. The other side of that coin is working on strategies to encourage staff to adopt more secure behaviours in such a way that it becomes a habit that functions even when we are removed from all of the reminders and checks that come from working around other people. The most effective way to do this is to examine the entire process of behaviour change, plan for all of the challenges and issues that might occur along the way, and craft our message accordingly. One way to do this is by working through a model like the Path to Habit as shown in the next diagram, and planning our actions at each stage.

DOI: 10.1201/9781003194583-6

The Path to Habit Model

It is easy to think that all it will take to change a person's behaviour is education. Surely, if we explain a risk and why we need them to change their behaviour to counter that risk, then they will take that on board, change their behaviour and eventually develop the new habit. But it is not as simple as that. Let's consider each stage in turn.

Explanation – This is the point at which the form and potential impact of the risk is identified and explained. The more the person understands this information, the more likely it is that they will change their behaviour in the desired way. Making sure that staff members are informed about the risks that apply to our 'New Normal' working patterns will make it much more likely they take on new behaviours and new habits that they follow whether they are working on-site or remotely.

Persuasion – Persuasion is about putting some power behind their new intention to change to use. This is the stage where those who still insist on using an approach that hinges on 'Fear, Uncertainty and Doubt' can run into difficulty. After all, control based on the fear of reprisal is only effective when the person perceives themselves at risk of being caught. Relying on this mechanism for your information security has the potential to fail spectacularly in a New Normal where people are more likely to be working remotely and outside the range of direct observation by their supervisor. This is why I always recommend moving away from fear-based approaches, and towards an organisational culture of insecurity awareness and engagement. Changing the workplace culture means that staff are more likely to behave securely because the workplace culture persuades and encourages them to do so at every step of the way. This is why installing insecurity awareness as simple 'part of the way we do things here' can be so powerful if harnessed properly.

Reinforcement – BJ Fogg states that it is best to design approaches to behaviour change that assume that staff won't always be motivated to maintain the behaviour, meaning that required changes should be both minimally disruptive and regularly reinforced.

It is easy to focus on the early stages of persuasion, where we are trying to encourage staff to take on new practices, but we need to make sure that this focus does not fall away once we see that change starts to take place. After all, we don't want staff to constantly have to think consciously about behaving securely, we want them to do it automatically. We want it to become a habit, so let's look at that process.

Fogg states that there are three key factors that need to be in place for any change in behaviour to become consistent:

Ability – Is it possible for the person to do as we have asked? Have we considered whether the new behaviour is feasible given the culture, context and working practices of our organisation? For example, instructing staff to use privacy screens on their devices if they use them outside of the office will likely be more successful if the screens are readily available on request, rather than after a lengthy administrative or procurement process which could result in delays, missed targets and disciplinary action.

Motivation – Are the staff motivated to change? Most people will be more likely to change their behaviour if they understand both 'why' they need to change and 'how' changing their behaviour will make a difference. But even this may not be enough if, for example, the person feels insecure in their position due to restructuring or redundancy – both of which are likely to happen in the wake of COVID-19. In situations like these, we can assume that staff are unlikely to have the motivation or capacity to try and learn a new behaviour when, from their perspective, it won't in the end if they're going to lose their job anyway. A wise security team will be sensitive to this kind of situation and ensure that measures such as regular access control reviews and monitoring on the size and origin of documents that are being emailed outside the organisation are undertaken to make sure that insecure practices are not creeping in as people's focus is pulled elsewhere.

Prompting – Are we regularly using reminders or nudges to reinforce behaviour? Remember, these do not always need to be overly complicated. For example, if the organisation requires that passwords to be changed on a regular basis then pushing out reminders about what makes a strong and secure password before the users need to change their password may be all it takes to help them put these principles into practice.

Small, relatively unobtrusive reminders like these are what Tim Ward calls 'Nudges'. We've talked about these in a previous chapter, but it's worth reviewing the key components here. So an effective nudge should be:

Easy to Interact With – This may include taking steps to make it easier to complete the action (such as including a link to a file they would need to open to complete the task) as well as allowing the nudge to be snoozed or dismissed if it has arrived at an inconvenient moment. It is important to say, however, that if the nudge is ignored or dismissed, it should be set to reappear at regular intervals until the person has appropriately reacted to the nudge.

Attractive – It needs to catch the eye without being disruptive. Walking this fine line can be one of the most difficult aspects of designing a good nudge, and often takes a lot of trial and error to get right in each organisation.

Timely – Although having something like an annual 'Cybersecurity Week' in terms of raising general awareness within the organisation, a yearly reminder to behave securely is simply not enough to be considered as an effective strategy on its own. This is because the behaviours that represent or introduce risk are going to happen throughout the year, with new risks appearing at any time, we need to nudge people to behave securely throughout the year too. This is especially important if we are seeing an evolution in a particular threat, such as the progression from Phishing (by email) to Smishing (which is Phishing by text). These sorts of attacks gained ground when people were working from home and separated from the very people who might have been able to help them identify the scam when it first landed in their messages – their information security team! This is why having regular communication and nudges directed towards staff working both remotely and at home is vital in ensuring ongoing protection.

The End Users' Perspective

So far, we have considered what we need to do in terms of crafting and reinforcing a security awareness message in the evolving workspace from our perspective as professionals who are already interested and invested in information security. Now, it is time to take a moment to consider this process from the other perspective, by stepping into the shoes of the staff member or end user. The work of Gundu and Flowerday in their 2012 paper 'The Enemy Within: A behavioural intention model and information security awareness process' is, I think, particularly helpful here as it describes what end users need in order to help them change their behaviour.

Knowledge – Do they understand what the risk is that the behaviour change is seeking to remove or mitigate? It is very easy for people in security to become so familiar with terms that we forget that they might sound like jargon to someone outside our field. A good example is 'Smishing', which has quickly become a common problem which your staff may even have come in contact with over the pandemic, but that few would know the name for. Remembering to make sure that our communication, training and nudges are accessible to the common person is vital, as a person who sees a warning from IT about Smishing, but doesn't see an explanation of what it means, may not go out of their way to research the word, and so may still fall prey to the scam despite the warning.

Perceived Severity – How serious do they think the threat is? It is important to explain the potential impact of the threats we are facing as clearly as possible when asking staff to behave securely, different people will have a different understanding of, and exposure to, risk prior to joining the team. If the user had only ever used public WiFi when they need to download a book onto their Kindle before joining the company, for example, then they may never have considered the potential risk of using that same WiFi for working purposes. Understanding the user's perspective and taking steps to make sure they understand the potential severity and impact of taking that risk empower them to make more secure decisions moving forward.

Perceived Vulnerability – How vulnerable is the device or system we are seeking to protect? Does the greatest vulnerability appear when documents are downloaded to a local machine from a protected shared drive? If so, consider if we need to try and change the behaviour of our staff, or whether it would be more effective to simply alter the settings so that a sensitive document can only be viewed and not saved locally. This solution sounds simple, and it is, where the needs of organisations and users remain static. However, we've learned through COVID that these needs can change quickly, and many organisations experienced great difficulties in trying to adapt to the sudden introduction of working from home in March 2020. Many, for example, realised that documents which had previously been view-only would need to be accessed from home, and sought to mitigate the risk introduced through requiring users to use VPNs to do so. This worked, but not without difficulty, the VPNs that were set up to support pre-COVID working patterns often lacked capacity to support everyone suddenly working from home, resulting in slow connections for the user.

It is in moments like these that educating our staff about the 'whys' of information security becomes invaluable, because a staff member who understands why using this inconvenient system is needed is far less likely to look for ways to avoid using it, because they understand the potential 'cost' if they don't.

Attitude – How does your staff feel about their role, the organisation and the information security team? A staff member who has a positive attitude is more likely to change their behaviours in the name of information security than someone who feels overwhelmed, under-supported or unappreciated. Although it may be tempting to consider this as 'somebody else's problem', it's vital that we maintain positive connections between the information security team and the wider staff group. This is particularly important as we shift into this 'New Normal' working age, where we may well be asking users to change their behaviour quickly and regularly in response to new challenges just as they're starting to get back on their feet. The decision to dedicate the extra effort to make sure that the information security team is perceived as supportive becomes a strategic one: it is not just about keeping people happy, it is about keeping them safe.

Self-Efficacy – Do they believe they can make this change in a secure way? To use me as an example, how likely am I to have to write down a secure PIN code if I need to change it every six months? What about every six weeks? You might assume that six weeks is a long enough period for anyone (including me) to get used to a new PIN code. You'd be incorrect, as living with dyspraxia means that learning new PIN codes is a nightmare, and requires significant time and effort, meaning that learning a new combination every six weeks would feel overwhelming. This feeling of overwhelming might lead to take steps (like writing my PIN on a Post-it note) that undermine the very security that introducing the six-week change was meant to remove, which ultimately meant that the policy can do more harm than good.

Consider situations like these as you create your protocols. You didn't know I was dyspraxic until I mentioned it, and there's a good chance that members of your organisation have other needs that you may never become aware of. As a result, I'd always recommend planning *as if* members of your organisation may run into issues like dyslexia, dyscalculia, dyspraxia and so on, and accounting from these throughout. This, alongside a policy that encourages staff to speak to you when they have a problem rather than attempting to mitigate or hide the problem themselves will result in a more secure environment for everyone.

Response Efficacy – Do they think that changing their behaviour will really make a difference against this risk? Linking to the elements which I've just discussed, t's always worth to remember that people will be less likely to adapt their behaviour if they think that their efforts won't make a difference. After all, if taking the extra steps to do X won't really help, why should they bother?

Response Cost – What is the cost to them if they don't adopt the new behaviour? It's important to balance the cost of not adopting the new behaviour, with the benefits of doing so. Planning out this aspect is always important, as while we should always aim to 'pull' staff towards more secure behaviour, there will always be a need for a 'push' element to make it clear that there is some penalty if they don't.

Security Culture – Is behaving securely 'just how we do things here'? A strong security culture is the glue that holds all of these factors together. After all, working in an environment where everyone always locks their screens, uses screen protectors and so on makes it much more likely that individual staff members will begin to follow suit. Social norms and expectations are powerful drivers, especially in situations where we are driven to fit in, to be liked and to be respected. A workplace culture of security and insecurity awareness, which holds secure behaviour as the standard, will call its staff to respond or face significant social and professional costs. A benefit of this can be that once the culture is in place, many staff won't even notice it as behaving securely stops being a conscious effort and becomes an unthinking habit.

The Gulf of Execution

So, what happens after we educate our staff and successfully motivate them to change their behaviours? Why is it that good, motivated staff can leave a training session with every intention of adopting a new behaviour, and still fall short?

They've probably fallen into the Gulf of Execution. Let me give you an example.

Lewis the Senior Administrator found the early stages of the pandemic incredibly stressful. The sudden shift from on-site working to working from home meant that his days were suddenly full of online meetings, leaving him little space to complete the things on his to-do list. It seemed like every time he came out of a meeting, someone saw his icon turn green and gave him a call. These were small things – 'just a quick question' his colleagues would say, or 'I just want to check how you're doing', and just like that his days would vanish without ever having a moment to actively do what he needed to. This left him feeling increasingly overwhelmed, stressed, frustrated and (perhaps the worst) guilty for feeling this way. After all, everyone was struggling and his co-workers were only trying to be nice by checking in. But the cycle never stopped, and Lewis felt worse and worse, so he booked a holiday.

Lewis returned from a week at a remote yoga retreat feeling far better than he had when he left. The food had been wonderful and he'd found the fixed routine full of silent reflection and yoga soothing. Importantly, the retreat didn't allow smartphones, laptops or anything of the sort, so there had been no guilt about switching off and stepping away. No listening for the unexpected sound of an incoming call.

He decided to keep this going by changing his habits at home – starting with waking up an hour earlier for some meditation and yoga. He was determined not to fall back into old habits.

Unfortunately, the same pressures he had left behind were waiting when he came back. More meetings, more calls and a larger pile of work. After he mentioned that he was getting up earlier people started trying to contact him earlier, trying to get their 'quick question' answered before the rush. Over the next few weeks, these kinds of calls swallowed the full hour, and his meditation stopped entirely, his intention to change smothered by the same tasks that had sent him

The Gulf of Execution

Motivators   **Deterrents**

| **External** |
| Management |
| Positive Re-enforcement |
| Visible monitoring |
| Security Culture |
| Good response to feedback |

| **External** |
| Lack of trust in source expertise |
| Scarcity of required resource |
| Inadequate training |
| Operational problems |

| **Internal** |
| Understanding |
| Self-Efficacy |
| Commitment |
| Autonomy |
| Habit |

| **Internal** |
| Intention to behave |
| Commitment |
| Tension between Task and Security |
| Perceived work pressure |

to the retreat in the first place. After all, who had time to meditate these days?

Lewis' new behaviours fell into the Gulf of Execution – but who is to blame? The answer is more complicated than we tend to think.

So, let's consider some of the motivators for staff adopting new, more secure behaviours.

Management – What example is being set by management? What expectations do they have of others? Does the management make it clear that secure behaviours are important, necessary, or do they talk about them as if they are a pointless nuisance and avoid following protocol whenever possible? Either way, the leadership sets the tone for the rest of the organisation, and we often see staff fall in and follow their example for better or worse.

Positive Re-enforcement – How are the staff being encouraged to behave securely? Is it easy to fall back into techniques that rely on Fear and Uncertainty when we want staff to change their behaviour, but most people respond better to encouragement than they do to threats or intimidation? Encouragement doesn't need to be dramatic or eye-catching, even just a few words of praise and appreciation will do as staff are learning new behaviours.

Visible Monitoring – If there is a way of noticing that someone is following the new requirements, then this can certainly help with motivation. For example, a clear desk policy can be easily seen with a look around the office when most people have gone home. Again, it is important that this method is used to provide both positive feedback and corrective action, otherwise it can quickly create a negative and toxic environment for all involved.

Security Culture – A strong security culture can not only encourage staff to change their behaviour, when necessary, it can also guide newcomers into good practices and prepare them for any future changes to the protocol. If certain secure behaviours are commonly followed in an organisation, it is more likely that even temporary staff and outside contractors will fall into line, simply by following the example of others.

Good Response to Feedback – As a consultant, I am often working in organisations that are new to me, I am always aware of the power of listening to feedback. It's common for us to devise our security plans and protocols in isolation from the people we will need to use them. After all, our job is to look at the threat, develop the plan and then action it. All they need to do is follow it, right?

Wrong.

It's vital that we listen to staff when we introduce new procedures, and that we follow up on feedback. We need staff to feel able to tell us if there are 'teething problems', or if a particular setting is making something almost impossible in a secure way while still meeting targets. By following up on this feedback regularly and making every effort to mitigate the nuisance factor we introduce, we make it more likely that staff will adopt secure behaviours either because we have fixed the issue that made them problematic or because they understand that we *would if we could*, and that we wouldn't be asking them to put up with the extra burden if it wasn't important. This principle of collaboration rather than conflict helps to promote the idea of a security culture whereby all staff are working together to keep data safe, rather than following rules that are set and enforced.

Self-efficacy – Staff who feel capable of making a change that will be effective in mitigating the threat are more likely to follow through on making that change. This may sound simple, but the links between these factors can be delicate. Some of the issues around mask-wearing during COVID show this clearly, as the message about a necessary change in behaviour (wearing a mask) was undermined by questions about whether masks would really make a difference if other factors, such as ventilation, were not in place. As a result, the link between capability (if people could wear a mask) and effectiveness (if wearing the mask was worth it) was broken, resulting in some people having lower motivation to change their behaviour from not-wearing to wearing, and ultimately doing so rarely or not at all.

Commitment – This is similar to the 'attitude' element in the road to behavioural intent. If a person is determined to make a change then they are more likely to do so, as long as they have access to the tools, skills and opportunity to change. Creating this commitment can be difficult, however, as it requires us to craft messages that resonate with individual staff members on a personal and professional level. We'll talk about this in some detail later.

Habit – It is the 'gold standard' for secure behaviour. If a behaviour becomes a habit, we no longer need to rely on staff remembering to complete a particular action as they will do it automatically, and often without thinking. Habits form the foundation of our workplace culture, and helping staff develop good habits around information security and insecurity awareness is one of our most important goals as security professionals.

Autonomy – For some people, the ability to work without close supervision is an important element of their job. This can be useful, especially if it is made clear that this autonomy may be curtailed if they behave insecurely or refuse to take on new security practices.

On the other side of the Gulf of Execution point, there are those elements that can deter someone from pushing forward and changing their behaviour. Amongst those are as follows:

A Lack of Trust in the Source Expertise – If the member of staff thinks that the people who set a new requirement don't fully understand what they're asking, or 'how everything really works' in their role, they are less likely to comply with that requirement. Being seen to be open and responsive to feedback is one way of addressing these points of resistance, as it allows staff to raise relevant concerns and trust that they will be addressed appropriate rather than disregarded out of hand.

A Lack of Personal Expertise – This is an issue that can also come from a guideline being devised without full understanding of the circumstances in which it needs to be implemented. It's why we touched on the importance of understanding the actual knowledge and skill level of staff in previous chapters, because requiring behaviours that staff cannot follow, or do not know how to follow, is a recipe for failure. This is why changes that require the use of new software or new procedures should always be accompanied by the offer of training and access to a 'help hub' or specified person they can approach if they run into problems.

Resource Scarcity – If an organisation decides that data would be better protected if staff had privacy screens on both desktop and mobile computers and devices, then they need to ensure that the resource is available and, on every machine, before the requirement comes into force. If new staff, or staff who have to change their machines or screens, experience delays in accessing resources, they will be less likely to develop good habits about using them in the long run.

Inappropriate Training – Security awareness training has improved significantly over the last decade or so, but we still have a long way to go. Organisations should always consider both the content and the audience for their training, and make sure that they're delivering relevant and up-to-date information that is useful to the person sitting in front of them *each and every time*. Training needs to be in a form that is meaningful to the person and draws clear links between the content delivered and the work they are doing if they are to take it in as meaningful information. Training sessions which are out of date, inappropriate to the user or delivered in a way that doesn't make it clear how this applies to the work they are doing will reduce people's engagement and make the job of the information security team more difficult in the long run.

Intention to Behave – This seems simple but if a person has a bad relationship with the organisation, then not only are they unlikely to want to make an effort to change their behaviour, they may become an 'inside risk' as they make a conscious decision to undermine the security that others are working with. These situations should be picked up by an employee's line manager, or flagged through their failure to complete mandatory training, with significant efforts made to try and address the issues that are causing this behaviour and the risks it represents.

Lack of Commitment – One of the hardest situations to manage in any organisation is when changes need to be made during a time of restructuring or change. Staff who are stressed about the future of their job are more likely to make mistakes, including their secure working. It would also be expected that the security culture of the organisation may diminish as individual commitment falls. It might be tempting to suggest that the security team should reduce their demands during this time, but the opposite is true. While secure working may be a long way down the list of concerns of one employee, leading to mistakes, the situation may drive another to deliberately break secure working practices to provide information to a rival organisation as they search for a new position. This is why periods of disruption should include more careful monitoring of access controls on secure systems to make sure that, for example, a member of staff who is released from their contract loses access to the system as soon as their contract expires at 5 pm on Friday, rather than waiting to remove it on Monday morning.

Tension Between Task and Security – This is a critical aspect that should be considered before any protocol or process is rolled out. Where there is a conflict between completing a task on time and to the standard required and working to maximise security awareness and behaviour, people will almost always choose to meet their objectives over delaying them. This is especially true if there is a culture of insecurity within the organisation, where, for example, issues with a VPN are not considered as valid reasons for delayed delivery of a document if 'everyone else found a way to get around the problem'.

Perceived Pressure – This sits with the previous point, except that the tension comes not from a conflict between the task and the security procedure but the social and emotional pressure experienced by the employee. We are more likely to see people cutting corners and falling back on insecure practices when they are under pressure, for example, especially if taking the extra steps to be secure is seen as taking too long for too little reward. Importantly, it doesn't matter if the pressure is 'real' or not. A person who feels stressed and under pressure is more likely to make risky decisions and have a harder time identifying the right path of action than one who is not. Managing these situations is difficult, not least because of the complexity of perceived pressure, so we will discuss it further in Chapter 7.

Making It Matter

Developing a security culture that supports and sustains sound operational practice from security and awareness is not easy, but it is more important than ever as we move towards a 'New Normal' of flexible, blended and seemingly ever-changing working patterns.

It's vital that we work alongside the staff we support and ensure that our security messages are made relevant to staff working in the office, at home or some combination of the two. This will require a great deal of effort on our part – changes to training, to protocol and to our own habits of working to make sure that we are easy to reach and available to staff when they have questions about behaving securely. We have to be prepared to respond to the changing needs of our workforce as the situation continues to change and evolve. Only then can we effectively guide and create the security-aware culture that will, ultimately, become the foundation of securing our organisations from digital threats.

6

THE CHALLENGES OF THE COVID YEARS AND THE 'NEW NORMAL'

Managing Your Staff

Introduction

Most managers learn their craft by a combination of experience and training. Even the best generally takes a long time to learn how to lead effectively without apparent effort.

When COVID dispersed the workforce, there was no training. There weren't even older members of staff who had experienced something similar in the past. This was new, and for most, uneven ground. Where did existing practices need adaptation? And where were new processes needed to provide staff, including managers, with support?

Add that to the challenges of having staff working in a largely unmonitored environment and you have the recipe for stress not least because working practices were having to change quickly, while not risking any data that was being processed.

Clear communication in crisis is key to navigating it successfully. When we read statements like these, it's easy to think about communication (often in terms of instructions) as flowing in one direction – from the top of the hierarchy to the bottom. But if COVID has taught us anything about working during a crisis, it is that it's vital to facilitate communication in all directions – top-down, bottom-up and side to side.

Have you ever taken a moment to sit and think, deeply, viscerally, about how different the experience of living through COVID-19 would have been if it had happened 10, 15 or 20 years ago?

The technologies that not only made it possible for us to work from home but to shop for food, watch an almost unlimited selection of

DOI: 10.1201/9781003194583-7

television shows and movies, and stay connected with friends and family, are all relatively new when we really think about it. It's not that long ago that video calls with multiple people would have been almost impossible – let alone achievable through software that was easy enough for inexperienced users to use with limited assistance. Yet that is what we had. That is how grandparents met new grandchildren, how children attended school and how we conducted many of our meetings for almost two years.

Many of us working in desk-based positions were able to shift (relatively) easily from working at a desk in the office to working at home using our own WiFi. I worked with four different organisations during the lockdown period, all without leaving my home. I don't think any of us could have predicted the huge changes we would experience, or how COVID would transform the way we worked. Perhaps if the lockdown had lasted the six weeks or so we all expected, then things would more or less return to the way it was, with a bit of catching up to do and lots of meetings. Perhaps there would be no 'New Normal'. But as time went on, it became clear that some aspects of the way we worked were forever changed and that we were now all in a world of new challenges, new restrictions and very little idea of how to manage them.

We quickly found that, for example, while we could meet together online, online meetings were tiring in a way that in-person meetings were not, and difficult to use for workshopping ideas or catching up informally. Now managers had to figure out how to monitor the mood and welfare of their staff without seeing them in person, without necessarily knowing the situation they were attempting to work in. Did they have stable internet, a dedicated desk, and a quiet room to use, or were they sat at an ironing board with a seven-year-old laptop praying the WiFi could handle a meeting where more than three people had their video turned on? It was hard to know, and harder still to address.

This is when I noticed a new emphasis on work–life balance being echoed through all of the organisations I worked in. Rather than talking about punishments if people left their desks when they should be working, managers started to encourage taking a break from the screen *before* getting a headache, and the importance of reaching out for support if people were struggling. These were concepts that were familiar, but rare to hear talked about seriously before COVID – yet now they're part of the fabric of how we manage working in the New Normal.

Yes, they have been managing people through COVID, in most cases entirely virtually, but that was always going to be finite, it was always going to come to an end, but what took a while to realise was that the differences that were required to manage online were the start of the new age of management.

The Video Challenges

Working virtually has always been a challenge. I was privileged to be part of a working group which between 2018 and 2020 created the ASA Guidance Standard for Security Awareness – the first of its kind. Work was divided between writing the text and frequent virtual meetings comprising of between 20 and 30 people at a time, each calling in from different places across the world. During this time, we faced many challenges – difficulties with workshopping ideas, issues with lag, with software updates and with the sheer practical task of editing a document together line by line. At the time, this was one of the most challenging and frustrating experiences of collaborative working I'd ever experienced and I wished that we'd simply been given the opportunity to hole up in a hotel together for a week instead.

I wish I knew then how familiar that situation would become once COVID hit – I'd surely have made a fortune on stickers and flash cards saying "You're on Mute!" if I'd had such a head start on the market!

There's no denying that video calls are exhausting. Maintaining focus and successfully working collaboratively over video takes an entirely different mindset and set of strategies than when we are physically together and we've learned a lot over these last years of the pandemic.

Teamwork – One of the work approaches that has been most impacted by working from home has been teamwork. This is especially where the team is creatively focused. If you are 'brainstorming' an idea in a physical meeting, members of the group can break off spontaneously or talk across each other. This is not acceptable in a video platform, however, as most will allow only one speaker at a time while simultaneously hiding lack of the visual cues making it easy to focus on one person. It must be said that the development of software that allows us to share a single digital 'whiteboard' has helped somewhat, as have other tools, but these are a poor imitation of being physically together.

Another problem with online meetings is that the quieter group members may find it more difficult to 'take the spotlight' and make themselves heard. Of course, this can be an issue in face-to-face situations too, but it's often easier to catch the eye of the facilitator, or mention ideas in passing than it is to stop the digital conversation and speak out. This, in turn, requires new strategies and approaches by coordinators and managers alike, and so the evolution of remote working continues.

It's important to remember that adapting to include quieter members of the team isn't a luxury, either. Studies into group or team dynamics have long recognised the different roles that individuals can play within a team: with Belbin (1981) being one of my favourites to use in a workplace setting. Belbin's model introduced nine different types of workers that comprised the most effective team including the 'Coordinator', who was usually the Chair, bringing ideas together, the 'Shaper' who has bags of passion and can be forceful in putting forward their ideas and the 'Completer-Finisher' who can be focused on detail and therefore useful for identifying errors in the preparation of a deliverer. It's easy to say that all of these types of workers can function just as well over video as they can in person – but after two years of COVID, we know that isn't always the case. Worse still, assuming that all of our team can work equally effectively over video risks losing key contributions from team members who fall into the 'The Plant'. This, in turn, creates problems as the Plant is often creative and a good problem solver, but can feel they don't want to push past the more energetic characters to make their points known without support from others. When we work in virtual spaces, those taking on the role of 'Coordinator' may find it more difficult to see when the 'Plant' is thinking, and when they're ready to contribute. This, in turn, may lead to the Plant not having the opportunity to be heard *at all*, meaning their ideas are lost while any problems they have identified remain unchallenged.

Another important aspect of group work is the binding of the members of the group. People need to get to know each other in order to work effectively together, and while this could happen organically in a physical workplace while making coffee or waiting for a meeting to start, these opportunities are lost in digital spaces. Indeed, bringing the team together and fostering these relationships is often one of the main drivers behind moving from a fully remote model to a hybrid working arrangement as we move into the New Normal.

One of the key elements of teamwork is the establishment of group norms that is the development of often unspoken agreements about how work is carried out, by whom and with what support. They're vital in establishing how teams approach their work, especially problem-solving and other non-routine elements. Think about the first day you had in the last job in pre-COVID times, when you first went into the main office. There are a huge number of social behaviours we have to learn from how quiet people expect the lunch break room to be, the use of mugs in the cupboard and to what should be kept in the fridge. It seems trivial, but when you are trying to fit into an established group these sorts of questions can be important. Learning these unspoken 'rules' is one reason why the first week at a new place of work can be so tiring, as you are not only learning all of the health and safety and security awareness and other essential training but also all of the spoken and unspoken rules about what it means to 'fit in' in your new team.

Making sure these norms reflect the kind of secure practices we want the staff to take on board as part of information security is a huge part of creating the secure culture we're striving towards. After all, if everyone wears their badges and takes them off before they leave the building, the new joiner will soon pick up that this is what to do. If it has been possible to cultivate a culture of 'if in doubt, ask' about suspicious emails, then the first time they check with a new colleague should be told that it isn't a problem and this is what to do – even if it is nothing really. When someone joins a team without that sort of example led security culture, it is harder for such things to become a habit.

Taking Virtual Control

It is worth pausing as we move further and see how we can continue to develop the use of virtual platforms to bring groups together. As we develop work modes in these days of the new work revolution, we need to understand more about how we can make the most of the virtual platforms we use, rather than using them for straightforward video calls alone. This is especially important for creative teams that would tend to work together in very physical ways pre-COVID. There is little doubt that getting a group of creative people sat around a table with a pile of pencils, 'Post-it' notes large sheets and plenty of snacks is an effective way to open up to 'blue sky thinking' with the team so sparking off each other to identify and develop ideas – but how can we support this in the virtual space? It's not enough to simply sit and mourn the loss of "the old days" of working together. We need to be pushing forward to new ways of achieving that same collaborative atmosphere and meeting those outcomes in the environment we now find ourselves in. When thinking about how to manage this, I find it often helps to focus on outcome, rather than format.

Aim – Every event has an aim. Yes, every event. Even the annual Christmas party is set up to achieve a particular goal, whether this is to celebrate the end of the year, to bring the team together, to celebrate successes and lift morale, or even just to enjoy a night out at the organisation's expense. So consider the aim behind your meetings, and shift your use of your software and your planned activities to fit – after all, nothing kills momentum faster than a meeting that should have been an email, and nothing is more frustrating than a series of back-and-forth emails that could have been cleared up by getting everyone on the same digital call for ten minutes.

Objectives – Yes, we all understand objectives at this point, but have we adapted them to the modern virtual context? If we think about the objectives of an online creative session, then we are considering the deliverables that should exist by the end of the session. But it's important to think about the ways in which objectives can, and should, shift. A good objective is relevant, important and recognised by the wider team, which may sound like common sense, but consider how many meetings you've attended over the last two years where you weren't certain why you were there, or worse, weren't certain what had been achieved once you'd left. Setting clear objectives before meetings and reviewing them often alongside any requirements (such as checking particular documents before a meeting) is vital to having effective meetings that keep the team engaged in a virtual space.

Chair/Host – While having clear aims and objectives is a good exercise, they mean very little without an effective Chairperson present to ensure that the meeting stays on track without getting bogged down unnecessarily. How this is accomplished is, again, different in a digital space than a physical one, as it's more difficult to catch the eye of someone across a screen than it is to message them privately to bring them back on track, while the inverse is true when we are physically together.

Most managers who were used to working in an office-based environment felt that they had lost access to a huge range of the tools they used to guide and manage staff effectively when we moved into remote working. They could no longer notice those behavioural cues such as the way people walk and sit to get an idea of how their staff were feeling. In the rush to adapt their practice, some turned to software that monitored staff's attention during meetings by tracking their gaze and alerting the meeting host if anyone looked away for more than a set number of seconds. Rather than supporting managers and staff, many found these functions eroded trust and communication, as managers were alerted to staff members 'not paying attention' and challenged this behaviour, only to find out that the person in question was in fact, opening relevant documents or searching for information that was pertinent to the discussion. These interactions often took a harsh toll on working relationships, sometimes with significant consequences in terms of motivation and mental health for everyone involved.

Living at Work

One of the most insightful comments that I have come across with regard to working from home is that we have spent the last several years "not so much working from home as living at work." And this is often true: there have been many reports over the last two years that identify the fact that staff worked longer hours when they worked at home than they ever did in the physical office – and often with less recognition from those around them.

As security professionals, we need to try and understand the pressures as well as the opportunities that homeworking brings, especially as we navigate our way into a New Normal full of hybrid working and changing restrictions. Staff who are tired or feel stressed, tired alienated from the culture of the organisation, let alone the security culture that is woven into it are hardly going to make an extra effort to work in a secure way. This is why it's important to follow the advice of those like Ian Pratt, Global Head of Security for HP and "make it as easy to work security as it is to work insecurely". This is no small task, especially where the staff member is often working in their own environment without effective oversight.

For a long time, we have known that security awareness and culture needs to be holistic in the sense that it is part of the way staff operate throughout their lives, both at work and at home. One of the 'gifts' that the COVID era has given us has been the blurring between work and home, certainly for knowledge-based workers. Now, we can frame cyber threats in terms of both professional *and* private threats, making secure working practices as important for protecting their home life as it is in their daily work. This, too, is no small task for us, but we must adapt if we are to protect organisational data in an ever-growing range of environments going forward.

The Business Laptop

Many organisations report that their homeworking staff found that they were under pressure to allow their children to use their company laptops to do their homework due to a lack of access to other machines. This is a perfect example of how we need to respond flexibly to changing situations as, prior to COVID, allowing someone else to use a company laptop would have been a disciplinary matter within many organisations due to the security risks it introduced. So how should it have been handled? Maintaining a hard-line policy might have deterred some people from allowing their children to access the computer, but many more would simply have taken steps to hide this unauthorised use in exchange for their children being able to access their education. Better, then, to adapt- to follow the path set out by several companies and set up specific secondary profiles for staff members that needed them so that the laptop could be used by the child safely as long as they were supervised by the staff member themselves.

I've heard many accounts of this process being the first time some users realised it was possible for there to be different accounts present and accessible on their own home machine. This, then, became an opportunity to educate staff about basic security steps and how they could use them themselves as part of their daily routine to behave more securely in every aspect of their life. It was also a rare opportunity to show staff that information security protocols could make things easier, rather than more difficult in some cases – and that was a valuable lesson too as we try and move towards a more insecurity-aware culture across the board.

The Management Boundary

I used to have a manager whose favourite catchphrase was "I'm not your Priest and I'm not your Social Worker" which she used to remind us that we were at work to be productive, not to be cared for. While this attitude might have been common, and even practical, during the pre-COVID years, over 24 months in a global pandemic has made it clear that taking this kind of attitude towards staff is no longer reasonable or practical as a management strategy.

As we go forward into the 'New Normal Age', managers need to have a more nuanced stance on where they should make allowances for staff members' personal circumstances and where they should hold their ground about what they expect from an employee. This wasn't as important when work was happening primarily in a communal workspace where they could be easily surveilled by the manager in question, but the shift to working from home has meant a necessary shift away from the fear and uncertainty-based approaches and towards building relationships and leading compassionately if we are to support and maintain good staff within our organisations. There are several cases where this adaptation may be easy enough – with allowing staff members to step away from their desks to fetch their children from school as long as they made the time up later being one example – but it is not always so predictable.

Let me give you an example to show you what I mean.

> Rob is a single man working from home most of the time. He lives a couple of miles from his Mum who is a widow with delicate health. During the COVID time she started to call him during the day and ask him to go and get a few things from the local shop for her so that she could avoid leaving her home. These calls

and errands usually only took up about 30 minutes of Rob's day, which he simply balanced out by working slightly later in the evening. Once Rob moved to a hybrid working pattern that included working in the office twice a week, he found his Mum found this adjustment hard, and tried to make up for the 'lost' shopping opportunities by calling Rob more often with bigger lists on the 3 days he was working from home, resulting in more lost time during the day and Rob working later and later into the evening.

Now this is something that Rob and his Mum had to ultimately sort out between them, but Rob knew that he had to keep his line manager informed about the situation. The manager in turn felt that he had to give Rob some flexibility, but that he also needed to be fair to the other staff. This was a very difficult situation for Rob and his line manager, as Rob's personal life became a direct concern for the manager, and ultimately they sought support from HR to find solutions that worked for everyone while Rob supported his Mum to accept the different ways the world was shifting as the world settled into the new normal.

These are the kinds of situations we need to be sensitive to as we adapt our security procedures moving forward, because while the exact nature of Rob's situation does not necessarily impact us from an information security perspective, knowing that he is under more pressure and thus at risk of making more mistakes or struggling with cumbersome new requirements is absolutely something we should account for.

The Commute Opportunity and Threat

One of the things that COVID working did for many people – myself included – was release them from the daily commute. For me, it was just over two hours in total, provided I set out early enough to miss the peak traffic, and I can safely say that there has not been a moment in the last year that sat back and wished to be crammed onto a crowded train or stuck in stop-start traffic. This newly available time held opportunities, and I did think about taking a walk before work started as restrictions started to lift, while others began to fill that time with running, yoga, and other similar pursuits.

Yet with the loss of the commute, and therefore the reduced chance of data loss via shoulder surfing, visual data capture and over-listening, comes new challenges. Firstly, as we discussed in the chapters, there are the issues of encouraging staff to develop good security habits. This is especially important as we move towards more blended working arrangements which can allow us to fall back into old patterns of working and taking phone calls in public spaces as we move between spaces. Secondly, there are the issues around continuing to work from home securely as we begin to take meetings where some people may be in the office while others are at home. This may lead to more secure projects being worked on and a need to introduce measures like privacy screens within the home to allow for this without requiring people to (for example) close their screen or laptop when the person they were living with stopped by to give them a cup of coffee. Expecting people to protect data in this way introduces levels of stress and tension into their environment that we would tolerate in a shared office – and so we should be sensitive to that, too. Out of sight is no longer out of mind, for secure working practices or the effects they can have on the environment itself. Instead, we should use these changing times as opportunities to educate wider staff groups on the principles and practice of information security and insecurity awareness, encouraging them to come with us on our journey to best practice, rather than being dragged along behind.

Summary

It's almost cliche to say that the sudden shift towards working from home during the early phases of the pandemic made things difficult in many different ways. After all, we know, we experienced those times ourselves, yet we need to be cautious and avoid assuming that these challenges will vanish as the world opens up and finds a New Normal, because there is no going back. Working through COVID has fundamentally changed the way we work, and think about working in ways that we do not yet fully understand. The New Normal Age of working will introduce as many new challenges as it does opportunities; and we need to be prepared for that.

In this chapter, I have opened up many of the key challenges that emerged in COVID working, most of which will still need to be addressed going forward. We will need to focus on training and equipping staff to do their job in new and different ways as we establish a New Normal, no matter their level of responsibility. We will need to identify new methods of supporting remote working and ensuring that the tools that staff find useful (such as digital whiteboards and shared documents) can be made accessible in as secure a way as possible. In short, we will need to collaborate with our wider organisations and respond to their discoveries, as well as expect them to respond to ours as we navigate this new world together.

7

SECURITY AWARENESS PROGRAMS AND MENTAL HEALTH IN THE 'NEW NORMAL AGE'

Introduction

In the 20-odd years that I lectured in management, the only subject on any curriculum that I taught on that came close to considering mental health was called 'Personal Effectiveness' and considered the importance of a good work–life balance. And that, mostly from the perspective of the individual, not as a manager.

The fact that mental health is a subject that is more commonly openly discussed in the workplace is both a good and a bad side of the COVID times. It shows that the impact of the changes to work, and for many, the additional pressures of homeschooling or caring for a vulnerable person, has been significant. In this chapter, I have opened the subject up still further and tried to identify where security awareness can help by empowering, rather than alienating staff.

One of the most notable things that emerged during COVID lockdown was an increase in open discussions regarding mental health. People, even of my parents' generation, were publicly discussing the subject in a freely vulnerable and largely non-judgemental way that had only been practiced sporadically beforehand – and that mostly by younger generations. In looking at security awareness going forward beyond COVID, I am going to take a somewhat simplistic approach and identify situations where security awareness and its training in the broadest sense can have a negative impact on the mental health of staff, and then other situations where the impact is more positive.

I want to be clear from the start and say that I am not a mental health professional. My opinions are based on my experiences,

DOI: 10.1201/9781003194583-8

informed by colleagues and other sources I trust. While I have faith in what I'm saying, take it with a grain of salt.

BC: Before COVID

It was back in 2019 that I first encountered a workplace 'Mental Health First Aider'. I had heard and read about the idea, but I had yet to find how they would function in practice. As I reflect on that, I remember that most of us on that site were working in a crowded environment with limited windows; one floor in particular had little more than a narrow strip of glass positioned above eye level. The lift was sufficiently unreliable so as to be for the brave or desperate only, and large meetings would see the staircase packed in a way that you might imagine in a fire drill. Meeting rooms were often packed with more people than they could hold in comfort, both through a lack of chairs and a lack of ventilation. There was also – possibly related to the lack of meeting rooms – the use of the literal 'stand up' meeting, supposedly to keep the meetings short while also enabling it to be held in a corridor. These seemed to me to be a bad idea for three reasons. Firstly, because anyone who was not comfortably able to stand for the 20 or 30 minutes that these tended to take was not able to attend. Secondly, matters were being discussed in an open environment where people who were not involved in the meeting could easily overhear the discussion. Finally, the meetings caused an obstruction in the corridors. While it is true that the space used that I came across was to one side of an open plan office so you could detour around the desks, they were still blocking a corridor which is bad both from a Health and Safety perspective and because it made the place feel more crowded.

While this was far from the worst building that I have worked in, it was a building of its time, probably built in the 1960s and was therefore wasn't built for the modern requirements of space, light and decent air conditioning. Thankfully my colleagues there were nice, and a sort of 'we're all coping together' culture developed over time which really helped with an experience that was, looking back, pretty grim in places.

Couple the physical conditions with the ever-increasing pressures of the modern work life, and I would imagine that the mental health first aiders had not been instigated simply as a token gesture. I certainly know that they had to deal with at least one incident in the eight months that I was in the physical office space, and I suspect there were more.

Over the last 15 to 20 years, there has been an accelerated move towards open plan offices and 'hot desking'. On the face of it, both of these approaches meant that the available space was more flexible. In practice, many people found them stressful. There was always noise, especially in a situation where people were frequently on the phone or having spontaneous meetings or chats at their desks. Many coped by wearing headphones or earbuds piping music to them as they worked and that was often helpful. But, by its nature, working like that separates people their environment and takes up more of their cognitive bandwidth so they are less likely to be aware of someone who is attempting to shoulder surf their screen. Also, it isolates the person from the casual chat that goes on and helps to build the team and the culture. While this is fine from time to time when the person is working on something that requires a lot of concentration, to self-isolate like this all of the time could be detrimental to team building and fulfilling the social needs of working together.

While some of the more modern places I have worked have provided 'break out' areas where people can chat, these were often still in areas within the open plan area so it is not a less busy space to take a break. Even before COVID in many instances many relaxation rooms became meeting rooms as the push for these increased as meetings became a core part of the working process. I have yet to work in a building where there were plenty of meeting rooms so I would expect those rooms to quickly move from being informal to formal rooms. From a security point of view, it is noticeable in most situations where people chat in these break out areas mentally zone the area around them in the same way as I described in my earlier description of the 'Virtual Booth'. If the chat touches areas of personal concern, such as might happen when someone is feeling stressed and decides to step back for a chat with a colleague to unwind for a few minutes, that information may well spread further than intended as those working close by will often be able to hear.

Coming back to the office after working from home for so long, one of the issues that people reported was that they found the amount of noise and people a little overwhelming, which will take some while to adjust to. I will discuss adjustment in a later chapter.

The Mechanical View of Workplace Stress

Modern office-based working cannot, and should not, be compared to the pressures of working in 19th- and 20th-century heavy industry, such as mineral mining, iron foundry, steel production and so on. For most office workers, the greatest physical dangers they might experience would be on their morning commute. That is not to say that an office environment is completely without its dangers. People trip and fall and cut themselves and experience a wide range of mostly minor injuries as well as catching whatever cold or other lurgy that is circulating around office staff or their families at any time. However, when we look at mental health, there have been many people whose mental health was severely, negatively impacted by their job, profession, relationships within the workplace and/or the work culture they found there.

Mental health may be seen as a modern concern, one that arrived after computers became a ubiquitous tool that speeded up many work processes. One reason for this is the language used to discuss that mental health has evolved over time. Until recently someone who needed to take time off work because of mental health was often referred to as someone being off sick due to the 'pressures of work'. Considering that term in the abstract, however, reveals how strangely mechanical it is as a representation of a human issue. It implies that management of these pressures could work just like adjusting settings on a boiler; if a weak point in the pipework is found, a small tweak of the valves here and there reduces the overall pressure in the system and prevents the weakened pipe from rupturing. So, in human terms if sources of stress could be identified then the pressure just needs to be reduced and the 'burst' of stress avoided. However, as any engineer who has worked with steam pipes could tell you identifying a point of weakness or undo pressure on a system is seldom as easy as you might expect in practice. This is even more true when the mechanical illustration is applied to people. These sorts of terms are particularly pervasive in contemporary discussions of mental health – pressures of being a first-time parent, the pressures of caring and the pressures of studying. To me, these feel like linguistic relics of a time when our understanding of mental health was far more rudimentary and less nuanced. The major downside of this approach is that it implies that the problem is, as previously highlighted, inherently manageable; that there is always some easy way to reduce or avoid the stresses in question. This framing is likely why it was common, until very recently, for people to express the idea that someone with depression should 'pull themselves together' or 'have a laugh'.

Recently, I had a discussion with my dad about this. He was a successful construction manager and director from the 1950s to the 1990s and you would expect that what was quite a macho profession, especially in those years, would not have much consideration for mental health. However, I knew he had worked for a number of years with a man who had mental health challenges and I was interested in how he managed that, especially as the man in question was a site manager, so had a lot of stress at times. Dad said that the time when the stress was most intense was towards the end of a job, especially when the job had precise requirements, such as in the building of a large hospital, he learnt that it was best to either make sure he had a deputy who was a good site agent himself or move the manager to a quieter job when the time of optimal stress approached. While both of these approaches appeared to work, they both demonstrate the mechanical and situational approach which I would expect of its time. I am not saying that he was wrong, but certainly I see the 'turn down the dial' approach here. Incidentally, the fact that my dad and I were having a discussion about mental health in the workplace shows how far things have developed over recent years.

Normalising Mental Health

Some of the most powerful approaches to help those of us who struggle to understand mental illness have come from some high-profile people who have chosen to reflect on and share their experiences with mental health challenges. Not for attention, or sympathy, but in the hope, it will help the rest of us to better understand.

The comedian and actor, Stephen Fry said,

> *Depression isn't a straightforward response to a bad situation.*
>
> *To understand the blackness, the lethargy, the hopelessness and loneliness they are going through, be there for them when they come through to the other side.*

I find this quote even more interesting in the context of Stephen's famous mental health episode in 1995 when he walked away from a play in London's West End just three days into its run. The fact that he not only resigned but essentially disappeared, staying out of touch with his agent and many of his close friends lead to intense interest from the mainstream media. Later, he spoke openly about his struggle to learn to live with a bipolar disorder and said that having the courage to step away from that situation saved his life as he believed that he would have committed suicide.

As a sign of how attitudes have changed around mental health in an article on Stephen's departure from *The Guardian* newspaper of 24 November 1995, we find these words reported from Stephen Fry's sister, Jo who was his personal assistant at the time (and whose age was included, even though Stephen's wasn't), in answer to the accusation that he had left suddenly because of a bad review by the *Observer's* theatre critic, Michael Coveney:

> *He definitely didn't walk out in a fit of pique because of bad reviews. He just had to have a break.*

To further show the concern for Mr. Fry's health, they reported,

> *One thing for sure is that Fry managed a decent breakfast after his walk out. He was spotted on Wednesday's 8.45am Ramsgate to Dunkirk ferry, tackling a traditional fry up while wearing a beige suit and glasses and reading a paperback.*

Obviously, if he had breakfast and read a book and was able to dress himself in a suit, he wasn't experiencing any kind of mental trauma.

Perhaps the most high-profile person in recent times to talk about their mental health was the late Robin Williams whose fight ultimately led to his death by suicide. One of his most famous comments on the subject of depression was as follows:

> *I think the saddest people always try their hardest to make people happy because they know what it's like to feel absolutely worthless.*

The fact that Robin and Stephen felt able to share their insights, and charities such as 'HeadsTogether' is spearheaded by well-known people, in that case by the Duke and Duchess of Cambridge shows how far society has come in accepting the reality of mental as well as physical health.

During the COVID-19 lockdown, many people were either iso-lated even contained indoors with one or more other people. There were also many stories carried in the media that showed the pressure that medical staff and other key workers were under as they tried to meet the need for their work.

Long hours of work which for many included separation from their families. This was because for some of those in directed con-tact with people with COVID had the ever-present fear catching the virus themselves and take it to their loved ones so they tried to minimise their contact with their family. The full extent of the impact of COVID times on the mental health of many will emerge slowly as the pressure is reduced. But one thing that this time has done is raise mental health as an issue that is not something people can be blamed for suffering from. It is an illness, short-term or chronic, just like physical illness.

Work-Based Stress

For many, the time of working from home has spared them from one of their key stresses of the working day, the commute and all that wraps around that. Before the lockdown, we had a driving commute of around 50 minutes – if we left the house no later than 6:30am.

If we were later, then the increase in traffic would mean it would take much longer. Fortunately, our children are adults so we didn't have to find a childminder who could take them in early enough and take them to school so we weren't travelling in the worst of the rush hour. Needing to get children dressed and ready to leave, with all the work and kit they needed for the day, as well as not forgetting all the stuff I needed for the day was, as for many before and since, a night-mare. So, even from early on in the lockdown, I am sure that for some the fact they didn't have to go through the daily ritual of the commute, regardless of how far or how difficult that journey was a great relief.

However, new 'stressors' were ready to jump out at us.

In the early months, those who routinely travelled as part of their job were at an advantage of being well practiced in using the technology surrounding communicating virtually for work. For the rest of us, we had a somewhat steep learning curve. Thankfully, early on the COVID age available bandwidth, at least in our bit of the world, meant that

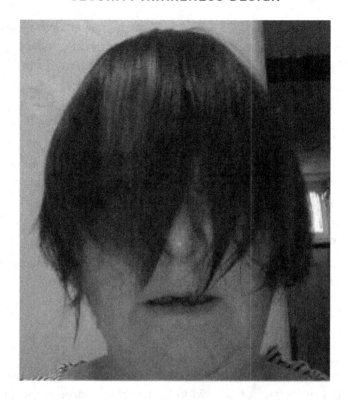

meetings hung and dropped and looking at shared documents was a bit
unreliable. For that reason, certainly in the organisations with which
I worked staff were spared the widespread use of video in meetings and
we were left watching flashing circles or odd profile pictures – which
were often not of the person themselves. Social and mainstream media
reported the increase in demand for leisurewear as opposed to normal business outfits. There was a suspicion that people were dressing
smartly only as far as was visible should a meeting use video. For me,
given that hairdressers were closed for about three months, felt it was a
good thing my colleagues couldn't see me.

But to be more serious, the inability to see the people you are talking to is something we are used to, phones being around longer than
any of us, but mostly that is a conversation with one person and even
at that it can easily lead to misunderstandings and unintentional interpretation of what is said largely because we are missing out on our
ability to see a person and their body language.

In the early days, I found it very hard to join in a group discussion. In a physical situation, people will lean forward, maybe even raise their hand slightly or catch the eye of the meeting Chair. There is the ability to raise your virtual hand in all the platforms I have used, but, especially in a big meeting, it can be hard to spot the little yellow hand. I found that I interrupted more, which I hated and felt almost instantly guilty for doing, but I was invited to the meeting so that, along with everyone else, I could participate where that was helpful, so I had to contribute where I could.

Also, in a physical meeting especially where a participant lacks a little confidence, the ability to look at other participants while they are making their point and be reassured by their encouraging looks when they do make a point can be a big help. Just think how much you can communicate with someone you know across a room or a table with subtle facial movements that can reassure the speaker that they have made a good contribution. In the video situation this was not present and for some that left them stressed and often not sharing their ideas.

Once video conferencing improved sufficiently that we could at least talk to a face, rather than a profile picture, other stress coming from extended periods of video meetings emerged. People reported that they felt an additional strain of being in front of the screen being watched, even filmed, for a great part of the day. However, in many situations, the acceptability of turning off the camera for some meetings is not universal and when new people join an organisation they may need to be told if the attitude to the use of video in meetings is flexible.

Norms

In social science, the term 'norm' refers to required or accepted behaviour within a culture; whether that is small such as a couple, or large such as within a country or an organisation. One of the important things that happens when a person moves to a new organisation is that they have to learn the culture and norms. And they need to do that quickly to prevent them from making a significant mistake. Back in the last century, when I was taking my postgraduate teacher training qualification, one of the things we were told about was the importance of picking up on the behaviour required in a school staffroom. There was, we were told, quite a lot of staffrooms where the different chairs had 'owners' or a part in the hierarchy of the staff. Basically, if there was a chair that was obviously more comfortable then that almost certainly 'belonged' to someone and we should make sure we didn't sit on it.

In fact, if we were to sit in the staffroom then we should take the chair in the worst position that looked the most shabby or uncomfortable. We may be encouraged to move over to a better one, but we would be unlikely to offend someone by sitting in the bad chair. There were also norms about how people addressed each other, how they dressed, what time they should arrive at school in order to be prepared for the children arriving and many others that the mists of time have blocked to me.

However, joining an organisation in the time of virtual working is harder because there wasn't the opportunity to observe colleagues working and get a feel for the pace of work, how much talking was acceptable at desks, how often you went for a coffee and how to approach the boss. During the period covered by COVID lockdown in Scotland, I joined three different organisations. Each one was friendly and welcoming, but it was hard to get to know colleagues and 'find my feet'. The last two had a refreshing unofficial approach in that I found I got meeting invites to 'coffee and a chat', 'Bring your own tea' and 'let's say hello' events where I just chatted with a new colleague and got to know them a little.

One of my favourite ideas that was around the catering arrangements that were planned for the first physical team meeting. There was a nice chat around whether from time to time, there should be a physical meeting that had a friendly element, be that cake or tea, fruit or whatever. In some other places I have worked, this sort of distraction would've been frowned upon in the past. It made me wonder if it was different as colleagues looked forward to a return from COVID restrictions.

One of those little norms that I have often fallen foul of is the little social 'chat'. Is it allowed, does it depend on who is talking, do you have to head out of the room and chat elsewhere? And there are many other norms that scatter a work environment's waiting to be detonated by the unwary. However, norms don't have to be negative, they can be things like 'if you have catered food left over from a meeting they should be put into the tea/coffee making kitchen for others to enjoy'. It seems simple, but we still have to learn that this is the way that it is done in the organisation, or within one team in the organisation. To a great extent, it is the habitualising of these norms that make a culture. As we build new security culture for the New Normal Era, we should consider norms a vital tool because if certain behaviours, such as the locking of a screen when the user steps away, are one of the norms of the office, then there is a smoother learning curve as colleagues will help each other make that behaviour a habit. It is not magic, effort still has to be put into working out what those messages are and how they are communicated. However, get that right and the behaviour implemented more easily with the re-enforcement that the norms will bring.

Indeed, one element of the journey to rediscover working in a formal work environment, regardless of how often a week or month that happens, will be the acceptable combination of pre-COVID working norms and changes that will evolve as people adjust to their return. This transition is likely to take a while, more likely counted in months or longer. Partly that will depend on how often people are present in the formal work environment. As security awareness practitioners, we should be ready to play our part in influencing the establishment of safer working practice for the protection of data on those harder days after the focus on the return to work fades away.

Return to Work

As we move through 2021, there is the start of what is often, too often actually, called 'Return to work'. As I started to write this section, I saw a comment by Lucy Brazier OBE which said,

> *Stop referring to it as 'returning to work' as if we have had 18 months off! It's quite the reverse. In most cases we have been working harder, with little direction, less time for ourselves and unclear boundaries.*

The workplace people will return to is likely to look very different to the one they left. This will be influenced by the ongoing requirement to maintain some element of social distancing. In many cases, there will be a greater demand for meeting spaces and fewer individual desks as staff attend the office for specific events such as team meetings and workshops.

Staff coming in will need to work out how they approach work in this new environment. It also means a return to some of the security messages that have not been needed when working from home. For example, it may be that many will operate a 'hot desking' system with few, if any, staff having their own dedicated desk. This means that desks will need to be cleared at the end of the working day. Where this is the case, the likelihood that sensitive documents be left on desks after the end of the day should be significantly reduced.

On the other side however, there will need to be adjustments for some with regard to the volume they speak at, especially when the subject matter is sensitive. In pre-COVID days, I found myself working in a large office and, probably because I was struggling to hear other people speaking with so much background noise, I found it hard to regulate the volume of my own speech to an acceptable level. I pre-warned my colleagues when I returned after COVID so that they warned me as I learned to adjust again.

The fact that for over 18 months most people have working in effective isolation, there are many behaviours we will need to re-learn, such as it has not been necessary to take care with discussing things that you wouldn't want colleagues to overhear, whether that is personal or official sensitive subjects. This is an example of where we can closely tie security awareness messages for work and non-work situations. Just as with the work on 'shoulder surfing' making people aware how indiscrete people can be in public places such as public transport and cafes will protect their personal discussions. This then can be slightly extended to make people aware that the same discretion is appropriate in the workplace too. In a situation where most of the internal walls in an office are thin, staff will need little demonstration of how easy it can be for conversation to be overheard. The fact that this is a good security awareness lesson for staff can be an example of how using examples that staff can relate to will help the learning of good 'New Normal' habits and behaviour.

Security Versus Mental Well-being Opportunity Cost

As I will cover in the next chapter, there is a range of security awareness messages that can be tailored to be helpful in any work condition including working at home and these can make the message clearer or more effective. However, there are some issues to do with 'New Normal' working that those charged with designing and communicating security messages need to be mindful of. We need to be considering the mental health of staff as well as the security. This is not least because if a member of staff is stressed or pressured they are much less likely to take security awareness messages on board. They can be just one more rule or requirement that is in their in tray and can be ignored. Indeed, if we make a process too difficult, then an overloaded member of staff might find a way around it.

An obvious example is where organisations still insist on a change of access passwords every six weeks. This has been set aside as counterproductive by many authorities in the Information and Cyber Security profession, not least of which is the National Cyber Security Centre (NCSC) in the UK.

The act of making people change passwords regularly not only places a cognitive burden on them to remember the new password and by extension on the organisation's Help Desk staff where resetting

passwords isn't automated, but it also doesn't significantly increase the protection of the data in the system.

Indeed, people are more likely to adopt a sequential approach to devising their password, for example, Password1, Password2 and so on.

For me personally, passwords are one of the few security 'good ideas' that can quite literally reduce me to tears. I have a learning issue that makes learning new passwords difficult. I use a system for building a password that helps me have a fighting chance of being able to consistently recreate the new password when I return to it. However, even with this, the first week or so of a new contract when I need to learn passwords for new machines and access points still carries a level of additional concern. I appreciate this is a serious textbook, but several years ago, I commissioned this illustration from Jim Barker to show how stressful passwords can be for me and many others and I use it here as a shorthand way of explaining this pressure.

To complete the list of password-related stressors for me:

Mandating Exactly the Format Mix – for example, at least "2 upper case, 2 lower case, 2 numbers and 2 special characters". My password building process allows for this, but not everyone's does.

No Special Characters – I have come across this several times and I neither understand it nor find it easy to adapt my process to this format without having to write down the password.

Don't Write It Down – Fair, but harder where a password needs to be constructed quickly and without warning.

Make the Person Who Forgets Their Password Feel Stupid With the Process to Retrieve or Reset Passwords Is Handled – As a user, I am a big fan of the software that allows everyone to retrieve or reset the password after answering two or three of the ten questions that I have already answered. A bonus with this is incorrect answers can be used (for example, answer as if I was my best friend) and it doesn't matter as long as I remember what the incorrect answer is. For example, except where I am required to give my correct birth date, such as for interaction with HMRC (Her Majesty's Revenue and Customs), I always use an alternative one that is incorrect in every respect.

In economics, there is a term 'opportunity cost'. This is where the person evaluates the opportunities or benefits they may miss out on by taking a particular approach.

After a nice meal, there is that moment when the person who is to wash the detritus from the preparation and cooking looks around the kitchen and decides whether to do the washing up that evening or whether to leave it to the next morning.

In my case, I often think this but, knowing that my mornings tend to be busy, I almost always wash up the cutlery and crockery from the evening meal at night, but the choice is dynamic. If we are especially tired it can occasionally get left until morning. With opportunity cost we are asking what is the cost, generally in time and effort, in choosing to leave the washing of the pots until morning. In my case, it would probably mean I would need to get up sooner or be rushing to get ready for work. We make that same decision many times in the day and throughout our lives from trivial things such as when to do the weekly shop to bigger decisions such as which car should we buy; how far down the electric/hybrid scale do we go while still having a car that will do the length and regularity of driving that we do. An important factor in opportunity cost is not only that it is subjective but also situation dependent. Let's think about choosing to drive to work or take a bus. There are a number of factors that are relevant to this decision: what time do I need to catch the bus in order to be at work on time, how long are the connecting journeys between home and the bus stop and how long the walk is at the other end. I might also consider how likely am I to get a seat on the bus, which is especially important if the journey is long. If the day is wet, then I will probably drive because the 'cost' of getting wet on the way to the bus stop, waiting for the bus and the last stage walk too may make the drive more attractive. The opportunity cost of taking the bus would be higher than I would be happy with. With the proliferation of bus lanes in cities, the difference in time of journey is reduced as they are not caught in traffic as much as cars. That is a key reason why those lanes are there.

Putting into an everyday example, it is easy to see how we need to reduce the 'cost' of taking the preferred behaviour. However, we don't always bring it to devising secure behaviour. I once asked a group of people how they could be sure that staff would follow a new process and the answer I was given was "because I tell them to." That led to one of those rare moments when I had nothing appropriate to say, not least because I thought "oh boy, wow" seemed unfriendly. He had a lot of belief in the power associated with his threat, but I suspect his HR department would not agree with that being a reasonable motivation.

Elsewhere in this book, I have discussed the importance of justifying required changes, well understanding the opportunity cost to staff is part of that justification. However, in this chapter, where we are looking at mental health, I need to dig more deeply.

While it is important to not overburden staff with security processes and behaviours because it could add to their stress, we also need to recognise that good targeting and delivery of security can actually reduce stress overall. Empowering staff to recognise risks and understand the defensive action they can take to protect themselves and their loved ones from them can help them feel just a little less powerless in a situation where so much work and life involves information technology.

It is expected that 'New Normal' working for many will be a hybrid of working from home and going into work. For many, the 'in work' part will be planned to cover meetings and other 'events' that work less well via video link, which will hopefully mean that staff are a bit less 'screen focused' than they would generally be in a normal working day. Why not try something a bit more interactive or even radical with security awareness. Why not have short 'Security Awareness Demonstrations' that are held in a common area that people can drift into or past? Setting something in an office means people have to step into the office, which shows interest when they may not be sure about doing that. These demonstrations – somewhat like cooking or baking demonstrations – that you find at 'Ideal Home Shows' could demonstrate setting up anti-virus, recognising the most up-to-date phishing or malware approaches. There could be a 'story corner' where someone shares some of the most recent security stories which people can not only listen to – so like having someone reading a story from online material – but also ask questions. And this would all be short not least because these 'in work days' are likely to be busy. There could even be a physical help desk for open chats about issues with regard to home or work security concerns.

This more open and interactive approach is something that may need investment. IT staff may need training in presentation and in dealing with queries in an effective way. Also, not all IT staff would want to begin putting into this sort of situation, and it is not something that should be forced on anyone. However, training could be provided to both.

Security awareness and behaviour is just one of the points that may cause stress as the workplace slowly morphs into the future. Let's be open to the positive ways that instead it can empower and build a positive culture.

8

LOOKING BACK AT THE START OF 'NEW NORMAL' WORKING

A CASE STUDY

Introduction

In trying to find a way that would allow for a review of the issues raised in this book, I realised that I wanted that to be in a practical context. Finding a way of doing this was probably the biggest challenge in writing this book. In the end, I decided that I would use another voice in a case-study context. I would put the review in the presentation of a character who was given the task of persuading people that working through these COVID times hasn't been all bad.

I then took that one stage further and used slides to illustrate her points. The slides are intended to reflect the points made in the chapters, while her script is applying those ideas in the work environment. Doing this will re-enforce key messages while placing the ideas in the challenges of daily work.

It has been a couple of years since we all emerged from nearly two years of working from home, blinking and disorientated into a world that was not only unfamiliar but also changing and adapting under my feet. My name is Annabelle and I work in the cybersecurity team of a company in the finance sector in the UK. More specifically, my work is around promoting security awareness in the organisation. As I look back at the last four years that included COVID working and the start of what was generally called the 'New Normal Era', I marvel at the changes that happened.

Although we hope that such a challenge never reoccurs, there are things we learned that should not be lost in the mists of our memories. Therefore, I was delighted to have the opportunity to deliver a

DOI: 10.1201/9781003194583-9

Looking Backwards from the Future

Lessons we learnt about Security Awareness through COVID working
and the start of the 'New Normal Era'

Annabelle Cooper
Security Awareness Communications Specialist

---

presentation to fellow professionals that, as honestly as I was able to be, examined what it was like working in a security awareness function during those times; the challenges and the rewards and gems of experience that we should recognise and take forward into our future work.

OUTLINE

- Introduction
- The day we all went home – and what came after
- The COVID strain
- Preparing for 'New Normal Working'
- Building the New Normal Era

Although we are looking at lessons learnt, I felt it was important to set the scene. It is over three years ago now and it is easy to forget the impact of going home for a few weeks and not returning for about 18 months.

I am then going to progress through to the dawn of 'New Normal Working' and end with a retrospective look at what happened that we did expect and those things we didn't and can certainly learn from going forward.

Introduction

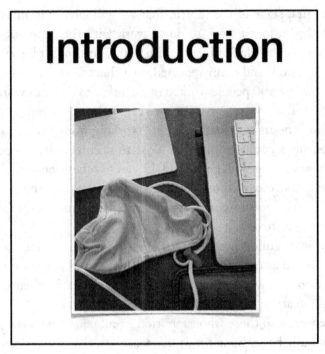

My desk and mask.

One day, in the spring of 2020, I cleared the drawers at my desk and headed home. I have a pre-existing health condition which meant that, here in Scotland, I was amongst those recommended to stay at home to keep safe. Like everyone else, this felt like the start of a welcome break from the morning and evening commute in order to keep me safe from this rather nasty flu that was circulating.

People left with so little expectation of being away long that the pedestal drawers under desks were left with various snack foods. Most were dry food, but it still made for quite an unpleasant job to open them up when we went back.

As it was, just a couple of weeks later, all my colleagues were also home. I was fortunate to be a consultant, so I had already made an area to work at home, because that was quite common with contracts. However, this was not available to all. Indeed, this search for somewhere to work led to an increased demand for garden sheds and other wooden buildings in the garden. Anything to get them into place which would allow work to continue as usual.

In the first stage of the return, that we will look at in more detail later, we had a lot of work to do to work with the adaptations that many had been made, and it was frustrating at times. However, as a wise person said, and many repeated, in a short time, we went from a situation where 500 people worked in the office to our staff working in 500 offices. There was no way this was ever going to be easy, and many worked long hours to try and roll out 'Working from Home' to a state where business could go on in as close to normal a way as possible. From those dealing with getting IT kit out to others looking after the IT system and those who were managers and supporting managers while they tried to support their staff in circumstances that for many became very difficult.

Those with children generally found themselves trying to be the teacher as well as being a full-time member of staff at their own jobs. They had to deal with trying to get suitable devices for their children to be able to access school resources.

There were also those who supported a frail person who was shielding on a daily basis. Sometimes this was with that person coming to live with them to keep them safe, or frequent visits to leave groceries or other necessities on the step so they could be picked up once they had stepped back. Again, the pressure of that should not be underestimated.

As you might imagine when almost all the 'Knowledge Workers' in a country move to have their meetings on video platforms the bandwidth creaked, and the platforms really struggled. Meetings would commonly have ten minutes at the beginning when everyone was trying to get in.

This connectivity problem also applied, in many cases, to secure storage where personal or sensitive documents were to be stored. These were not reliably accessible so staff, who were determined to do their work, saved documents locally or on private clouds. I know that was, and is, against the rules attached to the use of corporate machines, but getting the important work done was a strong counterbalance in the individual's risk calculation.

The point that this cartoon illustrates is the sort of password problems that I have suffered over the years as I am not able to easily learn a new password, especially when it has to be formed using a series of formatting requirements. When working from home this stress felt

'Poor Password' by Jim Barker.

even more pointless. In many ways, of course that is true, but there were still risks that we had to make sure that staff were made aware of. For example, as many people still use the name of their pet, favourite sports team or something that their close friends and family could guess, passwords had to be more carefully designed. Crafting that message so that as much as possible the message was seen as helpful rather than as a reprimand was hard – especially as for much of the time we were working in a vacuum of not meeting people face to face.

Before we go into those in more detail, I just want to be clear that I am not saying that staff were negligent or wilfully insecure in their practice, they just did what they could in the circumstances that they were in.

It was the responsibility of our team to identify these risks and guide staff away, sometimes we were more successful than others, but we found that humour, like in the cartoon, was both effective in sending out the message in a friendly way and remembered more effectively than an article or even much of the computer-based training.

If we consider the situation, many members of staff were working for a moment, we found that some were lucky enough to have a spare room they could use as an office, but many had to use kitchen tables and coffee tables, or just the computer on their knee.

Some of the staff didn't have their own computer at the time we all went home so there was frantic work across the world to try and find computers or tablets that would allow staff to work from home. A few people resorted to using their own computers or phones while they waited for the official ones. It was a risk and still is because that probably meant that information ended up stored on their personal machines, but then they had a job to do, so it was a rational short-term solution. However, this meant that we needed to provide information to staff around minimising the amount that was directly saved onto home drives or sent to private email. Unfortunately, the habit of working on home machines that some staff preferred had become quite embedded for some by the time we were able to get the corporate machines communicating in a reliable way.

I should recognise at this point the hard work that was done by those procuring, setting up and distributing the machines, and those on the help desk who had to support people getting themselves online and ready to work.

We also all had to become experts on being in home meetings. Even without the 'you're on mute' chant that cut into just about every meeting I went to, we had to learn to share screens, use virtual whiteboards and even upload profile pictures. From a security perspective, there was the chance of learning more about a colleague by looking at the room that could be seen over their shoulder. This is an amusing game but could have security implications if a social engineer who is trying to get onto your computer saw that you had posters from early 'Star Wars' films then that may hint at your age, but also give hints that could unlock your password.

We then had the problem of distractions: barking dogs, children who came into meetings – sometimes with hilarious results could be entertaining, but would in many cases increase the stress of the person in that place.

The COVID Strain

OUR COMMUNICATIONS HAD TO BE

- Clear
- Consistent
- Timely
- Relevant
- Respectful

Our security awareness core aims.

This is the point in my reflection where I want to look at time when working from home became the norm and preparations for return were put on hold. We had to accept that it was no longer appropriate to look for short-term fixes, it was about longer term working. This was no longer a little break from the daily commute, it had become the way we worked for the foreseeable future.

While this is about how we handled these years, it is important to remember the pressure our staff were under, including being ill themselves or having a loved one in hospital or a home with no visitors. There were too many who saw someone they cared about taken into hospital in an ambulance and never saw them again as they died while they were being treated. Managers were trying to judge the mental health of their team from their video meetings – assuming they had the video on, and the way they worked without any training for such a feat. Looking back, it was an almost impossible task.

Here in the security awareness team, we are always trying to minimise the disruption of a new secure process or behaviour as we know that this is the best chance to have people adopt it. Having a task harder by adding complicated or time-consuming operational security requirements is one way to increase the likelihood of it becoming a new safe habit. To that end, we stuck by the key rules we have with regard to communication.

Clear – Any security message needs to be clear for the person who is being expected to adopt it. This clarity must be in the description of the risk and the impact that it may have on the individual or the business. In other words, we need to be clear as to why we wanted them to make this effort.

This was particularly important because the individuals were not sitting with colleagues who they could turn to and say "I don't understand, why are they making us do this". When they were working from home, it was much less likely that this discussion would happen, which in turn meant that if they didn't understand they were unlikely to make the change we were hoping for. As with so many things, we generally found that linking the risk to a story of a situation where this risk had been realised – hopefully in another organisation – was the most effective method of doing this.

Consistent – One of the problems with providing good guidance around the design of passwords is that agreement of the best way to create a secure password has changed several times in the last 15 years or so. We have gone from one that needed to be between 6 and 8 characters long and not something people could guess, oh, and you needed a new one every six weeks and it could not be like the previous one so the next password after 'darthvader1' shouldn't be 'darthvader2' – and please don't put it on a note around your desk. From that, we tried for longer passwords with a sprinkling of numbers and special characters. In some situations, the changing interval went up to six months in some places – thereby reducing the number of notes. Currently, the advice is to use passphrases, which will be longer and easier to remember. Having capital letters, characters and numbers is still required by some systems, while others want no special characters. As we realised, when people were first setting up at home, there was the additional problem with home-based work that the password needed to be something that a close friend or family couldn't guess. We eventually came to the point, where we largely still are, where we encourage staff to use a password manager on browsers so that a more complex one is created and even the user wouldn't be able to guess it. The growth of this option has given us the chance to finally crawl out of that confusing and annoying situation.

Timely – There were security stories that hit the media that gave us the opportunity to send out a reminder. During COVID working, a number of these were around Ransomware attacks such as the one at Scottish Water over Christmas 2020. The impact of that particular one was felt by staff for a long time after as systems had to be rebuilt. This gave us the opportunity to encourage senior management to take part in one of the online workshops that helped to raise awareness of what an attack would be like and how to prepare to handle one. For the rest of the staff, we were able to push out communication around Phishing attacks explaining that if they saw something they suspected might be an attack and reported it, they would be playing an important part in protecting us from a similar experience.

Relevant – There are many different online resources available to us that we could use to both train staff and then measure how well they had taken the message on board. Some of the subjects in these training pieces are both well designed and interesting to staff. IT was important, however, that we ensured that staff were not being asked to defend against risks that were not relevant to them. In ordinary working times, for example, we would make sure that our staff who travelled a lot as part of their role, received advice around working in public spaces.

We tended not to use those communications for all staff as they were not relevant. However, as we will come to shortly, the message around these risks are now important to a wider percentage of our workforce.

Respectful – I think we all know that if we were to talk to staff as if they were idiots who exposed corporate data to risk just because they didn't make the effort to take care. While that situation may be true of a minority, taking that approach across the organisation will do little to promote good practice. During COVID times, this was a challenge we took extra effort with. We simply didn't know the situation in which the message would be presented, and we needed to ensure that we were taking the staff with us as we encouraged a change of work habit. We found that where a message regarding a risk was presented clearly and staff were in a situation whereby they were able to enter into a conversation if they felt that was something they wanted, the responses were more positive.

These core approaches were not singular to the COVID working times, the opportunity to repair any damage from poor communication was much lower, and in many cases, we were not able to be sure whether staff had taken a message into a habit anyway. We had to trust them.

Getting ready.

We started planning the route back not that long after we all went home. As we go through this I am going to divide the discussion into two phases; Preparing for 'New Normal' working and across the summer of 2020 it looked like we would be back by August, but then, as you know, it wasn't.

In the early days, quite a lot of staff raised issues such as building access keypads being a potential hotspot for contamination and also the lack of availability of suitably sized meeting rooms. The latter had been a problem before COVID, so we were not at all sure, due to the nature of the building how we were going to fix this, but we had to start to try and work that out.

Remember this was before there was a vaccine so it was a worrying time, especially for those who were vulnerable or lived with someone in that position.

The latter groups were particularly concerned that they might be forced to go back into work before it was safe, so we were dealing with some very anxious people.

Thankfully towards the end of the summer, the meeting platforms started to improve. If the meeting was not too big, it became possible to have cameras on more frequently. Also, and more importantly, file sharing on screen became more reliable and people became more used to do that. This meant that documents could be shared more spontaneously by more people, which reduced the need for sending them out by email, potentially being saved on non-corporate machines or clouds. This development was important where people were trying to design in a group – be that computer architecture or event planning or anything in between. And, as the time went on with no return in sight, then systems did have to be created and amended as they had been before. While you can never replace a group of people in a single place trying to brainstorm an idea, at least being able to look at a single screen was helpful.

Another challenge was the need to deal with the situation where people had moved within the organisation or left. While it was important that the laptops and devices were collected, it was also critical that they were either disposed of in a secure manner or made ready to be reassigned. However, the maintenance of a sound 'Joiners, Movers & Leavers' policy was critical. With the pressure on the system that came from both the working conditions and staff being unable to work as much as usual as they were ill themselves or had another member of the family who was ill made it easy to let this process slip down the priority list. I am sure that in the middle of the COVID time, the length of time taken to close down access to accounts for movers and leavers will have been longer than the guideline we have in place, priority was given to closing the accounts of leavers and making sure that their computers and devices were collected quickly. While I accept that allowing an established member of staff to hold onto access permissions that they no longer needed was a risk, we had to prioritise and that was the decision that was made. Once we moved towards the start of the 'New Normal Era', there was quite a lot of movement of staff especially of people leaving because they had been given time to reflect on their work over the previous year or so and were looking for new work as soon as the jobs market woke up again. This was another issue for us, and one which we significantly underestimated.

As the COVID time grew towards a year-long and vaccinations were rolling out across the working population, a form of return started to be approaching. We then had the slightly tricky job of trying to test the water in terms of the pattern of work staff were hoping to move to.

I say it was tricky because while some set out a clear indication of their preferences – sometimes with explanations, which was helpful, such as two days in the office, the rest from home, with a preference

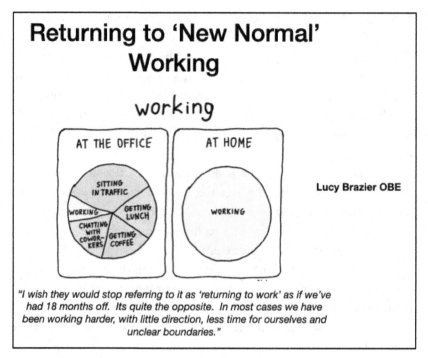

Returning to 'New Normal' Working

working

AT THE OFFICE

SITTING IN TRAFFIC
GETTING LUNCH
WORKING
CHATTING WITH COWOR-KERS
GETTING COFFEE

AT HOME

WORKING

Lucy Brazier OBE

"I wish they would stop referring to it as 'returning to work' as if we've had 18 months off. Its quite the opposite. In most cases we have been working harder, with little direction, less time for ourselves and unclear boundaries."

Working from home isn't easy.

to be able to step out at 3 pm to collect children from school. Some were nervous that if they didn't seem enthusiastic about coming back into the office, their job may be less assured. This was not helped by a number of the big corporate companies in London making public statements which were reported by the press as stating that they rejected any form of 'hybrid' working pattern. Staff needed to be in the office under the original conditions of their contract or be looking elsewhere for an employer. Some, as per the statement by Lucy Brazier OBE, found any suggestion that they hadn't been working to their fullest capacity when they were at home insulting. So, being aware that people were sensitive about their responses for several reasons, the tone of our communications had to be particularly careful and respectful. In fact, we pilot tested the questions amongst some volunteers from across the different teams to guide us. One respondent noted that some of the questions which those of us who designed them thought were quite innocent warm up questions said they found them worrying. We had simply asked how they expected their job to change when they began working under 'New Normal' conditions.

The respondent said that they feared that this might be less innocent if the person completing the quiz was worried about keeping their job. Maybe there was a 'correct' answer that would make them seem like a less enthusiastic member of staff who could be lost in a streamlining exercise. For example if they answered that they preferred to continue to work from home with only occasional visits to corporate premises they may be less of a 'team player'.

This sort of unexpected interpretations lead me to probably the core of this presentation. I am going to now look at what issues arose as 'New Normal' working was starting up and how they impacted us.

There were many issues that arose in the first few months as we returned. Lots of people have stories of what it was like to get back into the swing of some life outside the home. As the security awareness team we were trying to be aware of all the issues, but being mindful of where those had implications for security and secure behaviour.

Desk and people spacing was something we were able to anticipate. Facilities management worked hard at getting relevant spacing in place to keep staff as safe as possible from a COVID perspective but also giving people space to work.

We had expected that it would be possible to make good use of 'hot desking' as few staff had expressed the desire to be working in the office five days a week. However, in practice there was a problem in that teams often tried to be in the office at the same time for at least one day in the week. From a COVID safety perspective, there were potential issues of spacing, but it also meant that groups often

Issues

Expected	Unexpected
• Desk and people spacing.	• Desk and people spacing
• Meeting areas	• Teams tended to choose the same 'in work' day.
• Bringing computers onto the intranet for the first time	• Secure disposal backlog
• Re-introducing secure work habits	• Location awareness

Issues from the return to work.

informally gathered for work chats. While there was no enforcement of social distancing, it was still a bit of a concern when things were first settling down.

Meeting rooms were always at a premium, even before COVID, but now, when teams tended to come in on Tuesday, Wednesday or Thursday and need to hold many meetings. This meant that spare break out areas were often used and from a security perspective, due to the nature of open plan offices when teams were together chatting, the conversation could often be overheard by people outside of the team. In a couple of cases, third parties who were on the phone with members of staff could hear the conversation. In the end, we tried a combination of getting some movable screens to try and reduce the sound drift, and some reminders to staff to take care.

Another problem related to space and layout was that as teams were walking around outside of their normal areas trying to find meeting areas, we found that we needed to take more action to protect desktop screens from casual viewing by people outside the team. We already had those in the finance team's screens protected, but members of the security team and those dealing with sensitive personal data of any sort now needed screens. While those who have had these for a while seem to adjust, some who were using them for the first time took a while to get used to them.

Also, related to the layout problems, another we didn't anticipate was the matter of masks. For the first few weeks, watching the mask-wearing habits of people was a demonstration of group norms whereby an unspoken agreement arose which most people kept to. But we did find that where people were wearing masks the volume of speaking was higher as they tried to make sure they were heard through the fabric. While the solution was the same as that we have just discussed, it was important to be aware of all the elements that played into the overall increase in sound. We decided that this was a situation that most people would be aware of so we would take the opportunity to show them some situations where they may share more information than they intended – such as being in a coffee shop reading their credit card number to book a ticket – or even in a private house with visitors they didn't know well. We also encouraged an open discussion about risks people had seen at work or other places. This lets us get a view of overall awareness as well as the need for communication and support in their work.

At the end of one such event, a member of staff came to a member of our team for a quiet word. It seemed that they had been struggling working on their laptop which only had the single screen.

When they were working on complicated data, they sometimes found that they needed to print out documents. Because they were in a senior role they had access to quite a bit of sensitive material and were concerned that domestic paper disposal was not the best way to dispose of the paper once they were ready to throw it out. However, when they returned to the corporate office, they found that the confidential waste disposal bins were usually quite full, and they had a small bin bag full of the paper they needed to dispose of. We decided to meet this challenge in one of the two ways. The first was that we obviously needed to increase the number of confidential waste disposal bins and make sure that they were well signposted and emptied often enough. Even though the bins were often full, we suspected that many people were out of the habit of identifying sensitive waste for special disposal. Therefore, we would take an additional step of sending out a short vlog followed by a short article explaining what sort of documents needed to be disposed of carefully and we extended that explanation to cover personal sensitive documents that they may have at home. We then made eco-friendly bags available, the sort that had a flat bottom so they could sit in the member of staff's home and be used like a litter bin until it was ready to be brought in for secure disposal. It also had a gathered top like a duffel bag, so paper didn't escape. We decided not to put a company logo on it as we didn't want to attract attention if the member of staff was on public transport. Instead, we had the main company colour on it with the slogan 'I'm taking data security seriously' printed with the hat staff could have standing in their home office and then bring them in when they came into the office.

Secondly, we also made the little ink roller that you can see on the slide. This obfuscates information on a page such as addresses and bank account numbers and was expected to mostly be used at home. They did have a logo and were available for staff on request. This was a very popular item and certainly helped staff develop good sorting and data management issues. This was a significant request at a time when we had to be careful with budgets, but it was felt that it was an investment in forming good habits, and not so much when compared to the risk of a data leak.

BUILDING THE 'NEW NORMAL ERA'

- Personnel Changes – Joiners, Movers and Leavers
- Uncertainty
- Fundamental space issues
- Building a culture in 'the New Normal Era'

Changes we made for New Normal.

So here we are, all that was at over three years ago now. When people started to return, we thought we were aware that it would take a while for things to settle. But, maybe because we really wanted to get to a time of stability, we thought that once people worked out the right pattern of working in the formal office and working from home, we would get to a work pattern that was more stable. To an extent but there were other challenges we didn't expect.

As I have already said, the movement of staff was challenging. Access control, while essential to an operationally effective security culture, was not a high priority. But we learnt our lessons quite quickly in the early 'New Normal' days.

There was also a feeling of uncertainty which makes it harder to motivate people to act securely. Our greatest concern was uncertainty that led to staff becoming discontent. Nobody likes to be in a position where they are not sure they will still have their job in six months, but budget constraints, because the business market was uncertain, made it impossible to stop that without being dishonest with staff and promising that their job was secure when we didn't honestly know if it was. Of course, a discontent member of staff is a prime candidate for either deliberately working insecurely or doing so because they didn't want to take the additional steps needed to be part of a strong security culture.

Other issues I have noted on this slide that I have explained earlier in this presentation, but it is important to note here too as to some extent we still wrestle with them today, most obviously the problem of space for meetings. All we can do currently is to work with management to explore ways of facilitating meetings, including hybrid meetings, in ways that don't disturb other staff in their work. Some of these are technical tools but also looking at innovations around sound blocking and redesigning space when this justified the disruption.

Building a culture was a particular challenge. Although there had been plenty of virtual meetings, people didn't seem to have formed the same bond with each other. We rely on the cultural nudge of colleagues helping and supporting each other, not least in checking odd-looking emails – so "what do you think about this? Is it a phishing thing?" which are really important elements in security awareness took longer to re-establish than we expected. I think, honestly, in hybrid working, with some staff still only seeing each other at special events because their days didn't overlap, this was hard to avoid, but it meant we had to keep a greater emphasis on nudges to action that we had created and applied ourselves.

So, in summary, the time covering COVID working and the emergence of 'New Normal' working have been challenging to everyone. Indeed, you can see on the slide some of the core challenges for those of us working in security awareness. However, I want to use this last piece as a moment to acknowledge the work that ordinary staff have done to help preserve the security of our data. We lost a number of tools in our work of building habits including the help of other colleagues in nudging and reminding those around them to do things like leaving their computer somewhere safe when it was not in use for a while. We also largely lost the ability to identify and applaud where

Summary

Challenges	**Rewards**
Communicating with staff effectively about risks and threats	Using a more holistic approach to security and awareness communication
Maintaining a culture of secure operations	Gave us the opportunity to strip down and rebuild our approach to security awareness
Working in public	
Harder to identify and call out good practice	

Summary.

staff have made a good effort or have had good ideas to help improve our secure habits. But, at the same time, we gained things like being able to make more use of the more holistic view of security, so secure practice doesn't stop at the corporate office door. We have looked at advice for helping children, older relatives and staff working in their own homes to be more security-aware and empowered to protect sensitive data.

For me, the most important part was that we were given the chance to take our approach to security awareness and especially its communication, right back to basics and build it anew for the new world of hybrid work and the technological innovations that have grown to surround that.

None of this would have been possible without the support of senior managers and the co-operation of staff in all areas. It has been the worst of times, and yet, in a small way, the best of times too.

Are there any questions?

9

CARRYING FORWARD THE LOOT FROM THE HARD-FOUGHT BATTLE

This morning it is wet, and I am very thankful that I don't have to seat in commuter traffic in order to attend the meetings of the day ahead. Not so long ago, I had a boss who would not allow me to work from home in case I didn't work at all. I wonder if her perspective has changed in recent years.

For the longest part of the time, I have been part of the Information and cybersecurity profession, security awareness has been perceived as a 'soft' subject mostly fuelled by common sense. It certainly could not replace technical security. I have no problem with the latter part of that idea. I believe strongly in using technology to identify threats and protect against them, but when the technology fails and attacks such as phishing emails or malicious insiders threaten our system it is the human that stands between the attacker and success.

While some say people are the weakest link, and by some measure they may be, they are the final link. They are what comes between successful attack and successful defence. If they are weak, then our procedures and controls need to be stronger and those who work with them need to understand them better and build them as part of their security habits. If that fails it may be because we have failed as communicators, listening as well as transmitting. Although there will always be contrary folk, most will do the best they can, as long as they understand what they need to do, and that the behaviour change is possible while doing the job they are there to do.

The gift that COVID and New Normal working gave us is that we had to dig right back into our control policies and required behaviours and understand them and improve them – and then communicate with staff about them. We had to make those requirements work even

DOI: 10.1201/9781003194583-10

when we couldn't see staff work or even know the circumstances under which they would be working. The point of this book was to identify the useful, positive lessons and insights we have gathered through these challenging times. We will hear many stories, going forward of things that failed and the strain on staff, and I don't want to downplay any of that, but I want to make sure we don't lose the victories that were so hard-won.

It has been long said that effective security behaviours and controls need to put the least stress possible on the person who is trying to do their job. In other words, we have to combine making a process do what is required with making it a process that can be used.

Obviously, no matter how good the design may seem from an architectural perspective, if people cannot work with it, then it won't work. When passwords were to be changed every six weeks, it was common to see passwords on paper on desks or around a screen. Too often I have heard and read comments like 'people who leave their passwords in plain sight should be sacked – there is no excuse'. Actually, there is an excuse, they kept making us change the password every six weeks and some members of staff would have multiple to remember and literally couldn't. Solutions are needed to allow for that, but instead many are still focused on the point where the process failed and assumed that this was due to a negative action by the human, not their acting in a rational way of dealing with demands they couldn't meet. Especially while people were working from home, there was no way that putting 'Post-it' notes on their desk or even on the fridge door would be noticed by their colleagues or line manager so they couldn't be reminded. Yet, there may still be a risk from people in the house who should not have access to sensitive information and would potentially be given access if it were in plain sight. So, where possible during COVID working, many organisations increased the periods between password changing, and even automatic reset software, which meant that staff didn't have to have that embarrassing chat with the help desk.

There have been many other secure behaviours that we had to rethink to be functional during COVID working. Many of those changes have been carried forward into the New Normal Era and helped to open communication around security awareness and behaviour across organisations. It is not before time.

These singular times have shown that we have to walk together with staff to build a security culture that contains good security awareness corresponding behaviour while our communication is respectful, and helpful and clear.

If there is one message I would like you to take from this book, it would be that robust security can be achieved because of our staff, not in spite of them.

10

"THEY THINK IT'S ALL OVER ..."*

Introduction

Just as this book was ready to go to press, the new variants of COVID, Delta and Omicron came along to change things again. To begin with, I thought they would make little difference; surely it was just an extension of existing COVID working. But, as we drew towards the end of 2021, it became clear that things were not the same and there were issues arising in the two very different organisations I was working with at the time, and many more. While not as earth-shattering as the sudden move to homeworking, I found it impacted the operations, and specifically the security and risk that I was a part of in some unexpected ways. Talking to colleagues and reading articles and listening to discussions, I don't think I'm the only one to notice.

The quote given earlier is a reference to the last time the English football (Soccer, to my friends from the American side of The Pond) team won the World Cup in 1966. It was the last few seconds of the match and the commentator for the BBC, Kenneth Wolstenholme overcome by the emotion of England leading West Germany by 3 goals to 2 at the end of extra time was taken off guard when a final goal from Geoff Hurst sealed the score at 4–2 to England.

I know we haven't won the world cup, but this last-minute change has taken me, and many of those I work and network with, somewhat by surprise.

For that reason, I decided that adding this last reflection on 'New Normal 1.0' was important.

---

* This is a quote from the soccer commentator Kenneth Wolstenholme in the final seconds of the 1966 World Cup when England beat Germany. Some of the crowd started to come onto the pitch because they thought the game was finished. Then a final goal was scored, and he said "it is now!"

DOI: 10.1201/9781003194583-11

When Will It Stop?

When the Second World War ended, there were two days that marked that event: VE, or Victory in Europe, Day and VJ, Victory over Japan, Day. Especially with the former, there were mass celebrations in the streets. Even the then Princess Elizabeth of Great Britain and her sister Margaret went out into the streets, called for the King at the gates of Buckingham Palace and took place in a conga dance through the Ritz Hotel. In many hospitals, when a cancer patient successfully completes their chemotherapy, they ring a bell to signal the end of that battle. The problem with COVID times is that there is no signal, there can be no street parties or bells rung because there will be no moment that marks the point where COVID will disappear. A medical friend of mine tells me that, if the infection follows a standard process of mutation will become more infectious and less harmful to all but the most vulnerable. But it won't go away.

How then can there be a moment when there is a return to normal? When there is a bell or a party that is a signal that says that there can be a return to something approaching normal – or maybe 'New Normal'.

In September and October, people were getting used to restrictions being lifted in the UK. This was more noticeable in England where the wearing of masks ceased to be mandatory in many situations. In Scotland, this didn't happen so maybe we were less shaken when, as the Christmas break approached, restrictions were tightened again and people became concerned that there may even be a lockdown again, which would stop families mixing again.

In the work environment, many plans were being designed and discussed. Where, in September, it was a reasonable assumption that there would be at least a part-time attendance in work, face-to-face meetings and larger events were worth planning. Now, on the return to work for the New Year, we seem to be back to planning hybrid events even through to May and June of 2022. With security awareness where staff are going to be working, and how they will need to access their training and advice will need to return to be virtual. More importantly, we need to be thinking about a working world where staff may, on short notice, be confined to their home again. Either because there is a virus or other illness that seems to spread quickly through a work establishment.

I suspect that staff will be encouraged to work from home if they, or someone they live with, catches an infection which might easily spread around colleagues. We may even have situations when things like the 'Winter Vomiting Bug' become very common in an office, and everyone is sent home so the place can be cleaned and to protect those who have so far not caught it. So really, we all become mobile workers, even if we can spend some of the time in a public office.

So, what does this mean going forward? I believe there are four areas that this lingering pandemic pattern will bring to the way we work.

1. **Mobile Working.** One of the benefits of working from home and an easing of rules on meeting and staying with people has meant that staff may feel able to work in someone else's home. In my case, my dad lives 300 miles away so when I go to see him it is helpful to be able to travel overnight on a Thursday and then do my Friday work from my dad's place so we have Friday evening and all of Saturday together. Now he lives in England, but many of my friends have close family in other countries. Many of which need a longer travel time to reach them and so it may seem sensible to take the required computing devices with them and work from a desk abroad. This may mean that they are working in an area where data they are working on is not allowed to be shared. I know of one case where a member of staff started up their laptop only to find an automatic control to wipe the disc of the machine if it was detected to be used in the country they were visiting. They were horrified and upset because they had not thought their destination was such a restricted place. Clearly, staff need to be aware that there are restrictions and that there may, especially where data processed is sensitive, need to be clear communication of the controls in place, the reasons for them and a simple way to get advice ahead of their journey.

2. **Normalise Policies, Procedures and Controls.** Where these have been adjusted to allow for working from home, they need to be reviewed and replaced by more permanent controls which include security requirements as well as an understanding of operational needs as part of the design process.

3. **Communication and Support.** Before Christmas, I had a fascinating 'tea and chat' break with a lady who designs security awareness materials. I always enjoy listening to the way people consider different approaches to communicating informational messaging, but this lady, Jemma Davis, knocked all my expectations out of the park. She was designing materials that could be easily adjusted by the user to make them clearer to people with a wide range of neurodivergent learning challenges. This started at the colour of the pages the material was viewed on and went on to designing for people who find it difficult to read long paragraphs of script, find different fonts to be more accessible, find audio reading of material helpful or prefer short messages to be presented in talks – but again taking care with backgrounds.

When we all worked in a corporate office, I could expect that the Human Resources team would know the baseline situation that everyone had and could offer screen filters, better seating and many other additional access help. I have never spoken to an HR team or a security team about how hard it is for me to learn and retain good passwords when they change often, but maybe I should, but when I can't just walk into a room and say to a team in general "who can I speak to about my password problem?" because I'm working from home does that mean I don't try and get help? Maybe, but those of us who try and support secure working should be making these conversations easier.

4. **Mental Health**. It may not be a surprise that the uncertainty of changing restrictions is making people tired. An article on the BBC News website on 8 January 2022 talked about COVID fatigue, and they didn't mean 'Long COVID', they meant that people were finding it hard to look forward with a positive frame of mind. While this is not helped by it being a time of year of short days and cold weather, it is something we need to be aware of. When we are trying to get people to make the effort to change and maintain good secure working practices, the importance of making these straightforward and clearly explained is more important than ever.

I believe we also need to make sure we are not going to forget the messages about taking care of mental as well as physical health. We know that when people are stressed it is those processes that are difficult or take longer to carry out that will be dropped. It is therefore especially important that security awareness practitioners are challenged by this when they are designing business processes and controls surrounding security.

Through much of COVID times, there was an acknowledgement that life and working practices would not return to the way things happened before. There would be an impact of the working practices and general culture that would stick, such as hybrid working. But I don't think many of us expected the uncertainty that would continue and undermine the cohesiveness of groups and business, let alone security culture. However, these times do give the security awareness work the opportunity to become more closely woven into the overall business culture as changes are made. At the same time, we can help to make staff feel more empowered in their work to protect sensitive data at home and at work. Staff who are so empowered can be a powerhouse for positive business practice. Better still as they identify with the culture then people are less likely to leave the organisation and it is then easier to learn and carry forward positive as well as negative lessons.

This was a tough time to work through. Hopefully, the toughest that any of us have to handle from a corporate perspective. It is then important, I believe, that we can move forward with experience that will enhance our work for the rest of our career.

Index

Printed in the United States
by Baker & Taylor Publisher Services